Contents

Acknowledgements

I would like to take this opportunity to thank the following people who so kindly shared their memories with me:

Audrey Wines née Arnold, Evelyn Fisher née Baker, Shirley Symons née Barry, Vera Biddle, Arnold Beardwell, Jane Black, Pamela Nicolle née Buckley, Christine Castro née Pilgrim, Mrs R. Channing, Lavender Baskett née Clarke, Lillian Clegg, June Wolfson née Cohen, Betty LeBail née Collas, Jennings née Cordell, Kathleen Corton, Rita Kirk née Curtis, Philip D'Arthreau, Kenneth Dobson, Jennifer D'Eath, Tom Dewar, Bryan Farmer, Joyce West née Fry, Betty Sutton née Gagg, Jean Barber née Garnham, Rozel Garnier, Iris Knudsen née Gent, Frances Lloyd née Hardy, Edward Harrington, Ann Headley née Peppercorn, Enid Helyer, Doreen Ramsenius née Hooper, Ann Beardwell née Honey, Betty Hull, Walter Hurst, Nita Luce née Jenkins, Betty Judge née Jones, Roy Judge, Mavis Burren née Kerr, John Kirk, Doreen Last, Iris Tilman née McCartney, Miriam McLeod, Brian Martin, Peggy Mayhew née Masterson, Alice Bott née Morgan, Ursula Nott, Mary Facey née Noyle, L. Powis, George Powis, Christine Jones née Pring, Roy Proctor, Ernie Prowse, Iris Prowse née Miller, Henry J. Ramagge, Joan Letts née Rands, Betty Easter née Robinson, Eddie Roland, Clarice Ruaux, Doug Ryall, Archie Salvidge, Eric Sephton, Mrs Sewell, Vera Sibley, E.A. Roy Simon, Mary Kingham née Spink, Linda Toomey (ex-Stebbing), Joan Stone née Stephenson, Joyce Stockton, Margaret Thompson, Margaret Durham née Watling, W.J. Wheatley, Caroline Williams, Joyce Withers, David Wood, Donald Wood, Margaret Woodrow, Mrs M. Worner née Phizacklea, Mr S.A. Yates.

I am grateful to Andy Mathieson for the use of Stillness School log, and Margaret Baker for kindly allowing me to use excerpts from her father, Fred Bond's unpublished memoirs.
My thanks also go to the following who allowed me to use illustrations:

Joyce Fry, Roy Judge, Iris Miller, Doug Ryall, Phyllis Sewell, June Wolfson, Margaret Woodrow, Donald Woods, Margaret Thompson, Joseph Morello, Bromley Local Studies Library, Hull Central Library, *Kent Messenger* Group Newspapers, London Metropolitan Archives, Southwark Local History Unit.

P

EVACUEES

EVACUATION IN WARTIME BRITAIN 1939–1945

MIKE BROWN

SUTTON PUBLISHING

First published in 2000 by
Sutton Publishing Limited · Phoenix Mill
Thrupp · Stroud · Gloucestershire · GL5 2BU

Reprinted in 2000

British Library Cataloguing in Publication Data
A catalogue record for this book is available from the British Library

ISBN 0 7509 2537 X

Typeset in 11/12pt Ehrhardt.
Typesetting and origination by
Sutton Publishing Limited.
Printed in Great Britain by
Redwood Books, Trowbridge, Wiltshire.

INTRODUCTION

'Bloody Vackees'

During the final days of peace in 1939 a massive exodus took place throughout the country. Nearly two million civilians, most of them children, were taken from the cities, industrial towns, and ports of Britain to the relative safety of the countryside, using trains, buses, trams, coaches, and even pleasure steamers. For many of the children it was the first time away from their families, for some the first time outside their town. They went, carrying a few belongings, not knowing where they would end up – when a group waiting at a London station were asked where they were going, one child replied, 'We don't know, sir, but the King knows.' For some it was the beginning of a great adventure, for others a nightmare. This was the first great evacuation, but not the last. During the course of the war there were to be two more and, in between, a constant flow of individuals and groups both into and out of danger.

This mass evacuation was the result of planning going back to the early 1920s; progress was sometimes painfully slow, sometimes almost in a panic, depending on the mood of the international situation. It has often been repeated that the evacuation programme went off with no hitches, but this is more what was reflected by the widespread propaganda at the time, aimed at reassuring those parents who had sent their children and encouraging those who had not. But there is no doubt that evacuation saved thousands of lives; up to the end of 1942, only twenty-seven children evacuated from London were killed in air raids, a tiny proportion compared with casualties among those who remained, the majority of whom were not physically hurt but many of whom suffered for years from the psychological effects of the bombing.

A large number of the evacuees were from the slums and tenements of the inner cities; some of the householders who took them in were given an insight into a world of poverty which many assumed had disappeared with Queen Victoria. The outcry that followed led to the Beveridge Report and today's welfare state. On the other hand, many of the evacuees were given an insight into the world outside the cities, of farms, countryside, and animal husbandry, which encouraged some to stay there after the war, and left many with a life-long love of the countryside.

The mass evacuation of the inner cities was an exercise which changed a generation, if not the whole country. Using contemporary documents, and the words of those who experienced it, I have tried to trace the story of the evacuation, the planning, the first attempt at the time of the Munich Crisis, and then the real thing. Then came the phoney war and the drift home, which soon became a flood, but for many their evacuation was a more permanent affair and many were to experience both the problems and the joys of billet life before they could finally return home.

Boys from Rochester Mathematical School starting their own 'Great Trek'. Notice the gas masks, especially the cloth case on the left, and the evacuation label. (Kent Messenger Newspaper Group)

ONE

How It All Began

As with so many aspects of the Second World War, the roots of evacuation can be traced back to the First World War. The first air raids on Britain began as early as 1914, with London being bombed for the first time in May of the following year. During the course of that war, fourteen hundred civilians were killed in just over one hundred raids, first by Zeppelins, then by heavy bombers. The citizens of Britain, generally secure from enemy action for almost a thousand years, now found themselves vulnerable, and became more so with each advance in aviation technology, in an inter-war period marked by record-breaking long-distance flights by such people as Charles Lindbergh, Amy Johnson and Amelia Earhart, and air races, such as the Schneider Trophy.

Less than three years after the signing of the Versailles Treaty the Air Raid Precautions, or ARP Committee was set up to examine the problems posed by air raids. Included in the topics for discussion suggested by the chairman, Sir John Anderson, at its first meeting in May 1924 was the possible evacuation of sections of the civilian population. The committee's earliest investigations into 'evasion', or evacuation as it came to be known, hinged on the premise that London, as the capital, would be the principle target of air attacks. The ARP Committee's first report in December 1925 established two basic points:

1) that it would be impossible to relocate most of the activities normally carried out in London, and
2) that the nation could not continue to exist if bombing forced these activities to cease.

The committee pointed out the disastrous effect that heavy civilian losses could have on the country's morale, and that in a democracy, curbs on the movement of private citizens could not be too widesweeping. It therefore proceeded to separate the population into two groups; those involved in vital work, and those whom they described as *les bouches inutiles*, i.e., those who played no direct part in essential war work especially women, children, the aged, and infirm. This group should be encouraged and helped to move. The committee realised that this would require a great deal of planning, and it was therefore proposed that schemes be drawn up by the Ministries of Health and Transport and the Boards of Education and Trade. The schemes needed to concentrate on the poorer districts of the capital, as wealthier families would be able to arrange to evacuate themselves. Some committee members were also of the opinion that the 'foreign,

Jewish and poor elements' who lived in the poorer areas would be likely to panic once bombing started, and should be evacuated as soon as possible to prevent them undermining morale. If this was not enough, they also believed that after bombing the poor would 'flock' to the wealthier areas and loot them wholesale. The Office of Works, it was suggested, should be instructed to make plans for the removal of artworks, national treasures, and historic and vital records to places of safety – safe, not only from bombing, but also, presumably, from being looted by the poor! This early work established basic principles upon which all later schemes were founded, the most important conclusions being that evacuation was desirable, that it should apply to specific groups, and that it should be voluntary.

By 1930, the main plan for civilian evacuation still presumed that the centre of London was effectively the only danger area. In this scheme, the London Underground would be the main vehicle for transporting thousands of Londoners to the outskirts of London and, it was assumed, safety. There were no plans as to what these 'evacuees' would do once they got there.

In 1931 another committee was set up, under the chairmanship of Sir Warren Fisher, to look into ARP services. Committee members were told by their experts that, in a future war, 600 tons of bombs per day could be dropped on Britain, following a huge opening assault dropping 3,500 tons in the first 24 hours causing 60,000 dead and 120,000 wounded on the first day, followed by 66,000 dead and 130,000 wounded per week thereafter. These figures led them, inevitably, to the conclusion that evacuation would play a vitally important role in any defence scheme, and they began close examination of the problem of evacuating 3½ million citizens from various parts of London. However, the findings of this committee, reported in 1934, were somewhat overshadowed when the scope of the ARP was enlarged to include not just London but the country as a whole in 1934/5. This latter move culminated in the formation of the ARP Department of the Home Office.

The idea of evacuation was certainly not unique to Britain, and other countries were pushing ahead with their plans; the French Government, for instance, issued a handbook on evacuation in 1936 setting out their scheme. All non-vital civilians would be encouraged to leave the towns; those closely related to people who needed to stay behind would be evacuated to places nearby, while those who had to remain would be evacuated each night. The mayor of each town would be responsible for the evacuation of his town, and for liaison with surrounding villages as to billeting. People were to be evacuated by trains, trams and buses, and all villages and towns were expected to accept a number of evacuees equal to their population.

Life, and death, in the city: a children's hospital ward in Belfast the morning after a raid. (HMSO)

*French evacuation:
Parisian children
undergoing medical
inspection on arrival at
their new billets,
September 1939.*

For the next few years evacuation plans progressed slowly in Britain. Some work was done on a London evacuation scheme but the 1937 government booklet *The Householder's Handbook*, updated in 1938, gave only one suggestion as to what to do if war threatened: 'If you live in a large town, children, invalids, elderly members of the household, and pets, should be sent to relatives or friends in the country, if this is possible.' As with other civil defence measures, the onus was placed on individuals to make their own arrangements.

In spite of optimistic statements by the Home Secretary, Sir Samuel Hoare, government plans for large-scale evacuation were still in a very rudimentary state by early 1938. In the Home Office air raid scheme issued to the county boroughs in March of that year, the paragraph on evacuation read: 'To be completed as and when further directions are given by the Secretary of State.' An accompanying circular instructed local authorities to take no action until specific instructions had been received from the Home Office.

On 26 May 1938 the Home Secretary announced that he had set up the 'Committee on Evacuation', made up of four MPs under Sir John Anderson. They met for the first time on the following day, when they agreed to look at foreign schemes. Meanwhile, it was widely accepted that the evacuation of children should form the most important part of any scheme, and would also be the easiest to organise. J.B.S. Haldane, in *ARP*, noted that: 'There is one class of the community which could be evacuated at very short notice, and with very little difficulty. These are the school children, and particularly the elementary school children. They are accustomed to obey their teachers, at least up to a point.' One of the many proposals put to the Anderson Committee was for the erection of 600 camp schools in rural areas, each to house 500 children, with foundations laid for other huts (stored in sections) so that the population of each camp could be increased to 5,000 in the event of an emergency. Each camp would be allocated to ten elementary schools that, in peace time, would use the camp in rotation, for one month each. In the event of war all ten schools could be evacuated to the camp, with the advantage that they would already know the camp and the surrounding area.

By this time, the government was under continued pressure to come up with definite plans. When questioned in Parliament about evacuation on 1 June 1938, the Home Secretary, was still vague: 'That question raises so many issues that although we have plans prepared in outline, I should be very loath to decide upon any one of them until I felt that there was general body of public opinion outside behind it.' The Anderson Committee reported back to the Home Secretary before the end of July, concluding that: 'The whole issue of any future war may well turn on the manner in which the problem of evacuation from densely populated industrial areas is handled.' While agreeing with the findings of earlier committees, the Anderson Committee further proposed that arrangements for the reception of refugees should rest primarily on accommodation in private houses under compulsory billeting powers, with the initial cost being borne by the government, though 'refugees' able to do so should later be required to make some contribution. Detailed plans should be laid to evacuate schoolchildren, with the consent of their parents, school by school, in the charge of their teachers and at government expense. Such a scheme, concluded the committee, could be organised within a few months, and it pressed for central and local organisations to be set up to carry out the required planning, beginning with the education of the public on the necessity for the scheme.

Here, then, for the first time, the committee had started to address the two problems that earlier schemes had failed to do: 1) what to do with the evacuees once they were out of the cities; and 2) in a voluntary system, how to encourage people to leave. Many saw these, correctly, as it turned out, as the greatest problems for any plan – they would never be completely solved. J.B.S. Haldane argued from his experiences in Spain that: 'People are only willing to leave their homes after so much bombing that transport is partially paralysed, and they are only willing to give full hospitality as honoured guests to their starving and lousy fellow-countrymen after they have learned patriotism.'

On 18 June 1938 the Women's Voluntary Service (WVS) was formed, primarily for recruiting women to the Civil Defence Services. However, from the very first the WVS proved adept at turning its hand to any necessary task and in July its founder, Lady Reading, addressed a secret meeting at the Girl Guides' Headquarters where she asked for the names of Guiders prepared to take responsibility for local evacuation arrangements, backed up by the WVS. Next, the support of the Women's Institutes (WI) was secured, and a WVS Evacuation Committee was set up that included representatives of the WI and the Guides. They then appointed a County Evacuation Officer in every county likely to receive evacuees.

Early in September 1938, with the Munich Crisis brewing, the Committee for Imperial Defence accepted the Anderson Committee's proposals.

TWO

Planning and Rehearsal

In September 1938 Britain found itself on the brink of war. Germany laid claim to a part of Czechoslovakia, the Sudetenland, which lay along their joint border; the Czechs dismissed their claim. Both countries prepared for a war into which France and Britain would be drawn by treaty commitments. Defence measures were rushed forward. On the basis of the Anderson Committee report, a scheme, later to become known as Plan 1, was hastily patched together for the evacuation of London children. On 22 September a special conference was held at Chelmsford, where Essex towns were asked to take their share of the 2 million people expected to be evacuated from the capital. This included almost 45,000 to be transferred to the Colchester area, to arrive over a five day period at a rate of nine train loads per day. Four days later, the Government asked the WVS to help every local authority in the reception areas to carry out a house-to-house census of accommodation likely to be available for evacuees (in some places this job was carried out by the Women's Institutes). The survey found almost 5 million spare billets in the reception areas, in most of which the WVS set up an evacuation committee, working with the Local Authority's Chief Billeting Officer, to coordinate the work of reception and billeting.

At the height of the crisis on Thursday 29th the Government published its plans for the assisted evacuation of 2 million people from London, one quarter of them schoolchildren. Already many were moving themselves and their families away from the main cities, the railways reporting passenger

BROCKLEY CENTRAL SCHOOL FOR BOYS,
WALLBUTTON ROAD, S.E.4.

27th September, 1938.

Dear Parents,

Will you have your boy's luggage ready Wednesday morning, fully labelled. If you live more than 15 minutes walk from the school, he must bring his case with him on Wednesday morning.

EQUIPMENT (apart from clothes worn)

Washing things - soap, towel. &.R School Hymn book.
Older clothes. Shirts. 3
Gym. vest, shorts & plimsolls. Pyjamas or nightshirt.
6 stamped post cards. Pullovers.
Mackintosh, brush, comb. Strong walking shoes.
Socks or stockings. Story or reading book.
Card games. Blanket, wrapped in water-
Gas Mask. not needed proof.

ALL TO BE PROPERLY MARKED

FOOD (for 1 or 2 days)

¼lb cooked meat. ¼lb chocolate.
2 hard boiled eggs. ¼lb raisins.
¼lb biscuits (wholemea 1) 12 prunes.
Butter (in container) Apples, oranges.
Knife, fork, spoon. Mug (unbreakable)

Yours sincerly,

CHARLES H. GREEN.

A letter dated 27 September 1938, setting out the items that the boys of Brockley Central School, South London, should bring with them for evacuation. Notable among the items of food are two boiled eggs and (presumably to counter their effect) twelve prunes.

NUMBERING OF EVACUATION SPECIALS AND SUMMARY OF EVACUATION SPECIALS—*continued*

No. of Train	Departure Time	Stations		Arrival Time	No. of Evac- ted	To be cleaned and watered	Empty stock returns same day		
		From	To				At	From	To
Fifth	**Day.**								
82	8-45 a.m.	Paddn.	Penzance ..	—	—	—	9-50 p.m.	Penzance ..	O. O. Com.
601	12§38 p.m.	S. Rly.	Churston...	2- 0 p.m.	800	By S. Rly...	2-45 p.m.	Churston...	Exeter ¶
83	9-12 a.m.	Paddn.	Camborne..	—	—	—	10-20 p.m.	Penzance ..	O. O. Com.
602	1§ 8 p.m.	S. Rly.	St. Germans	—	—	By S. Rly...	4- 5 p.m.	Liskeard ...	Exeter ¶
85	10-10 a.m.	Paddn.	Dulverton .	2-45 p.m.	100	Taunton ...	3- 0 p.m.	Dulverton .	O. O. Com.
86	10-40 a.m.	Paddn.	Truro	—	—	—	9-25 p.m.	Truro ...	O. O. Com.
603	2§35 p.m.	S. Rly.	Totnes.....	3-31 p.m.	800	By S. Rly...	3-50 p.m.	Totnes.....	Exeter ¶
88	11-40 a.m.	Paddn.	St. Austell .	—	—	—	9-20 p.m.	St. Austell .	W Lon. Sdgs
604	4§44 p.m.	S. Rly.	Newton A.	5-15 p.m.	800	By S. Rly...	6-50 p.m.	Newton A. .	Exeter ¶
92	1-40 p.m.	Paddn.	Tiverton ...	5-25 p.m.	800	Taunton ...	6- 0 p.m.	Tiverton ...	O. O. Com.
94	2-40 p.m.	Paddn.	Kingsbridge	8-30 p.m.	800	Newton A. .	8-55 p.m.	Kingsbridge	O. O. Com.
Sixth	**Day.**								
102	8-45 a.m.	Paddn.	Penzance ..	—	—	—	As ordered	by R.S. Control.	
701	12§38 p.m.	S. Rly.	Churston...	2- 0 p.m.	700	By S. Rly...	2-45 p.m.	Churston ..	Exeter ¶
103	9-12 a.m.	Paddn.	Camborne..	—	—	—	As ordered	by R.S. Control.	
702	1§ 8 p.m.	S. Rly.	St. Germans	—	—	By S. Rly...	4-5 p.m.	Liskeard ...	Exeter ¶
105	10-10 a.m.	Paddn.	Tiverton ...	2-40 p.m.	800	—	} As ordered	by R.S. Control.	
106	10-40 a.m.	Paddn.	Truro	—	—	—			
703	2§35 p.m.	S. Rly.	{ Newton A.	3- 8 p.m.	400	} By S. Rly.	4-50 p.m.	Paignton	Exeter ¶
			{ Torquay ..	3-35 p.m.	400				
108	11-40 a.m.	Paddn.	Penryn	—	—	—	As ordered	by R.S. Control.	
704	4†44 p.m.	S. Rly.	Newton A. .	5-15 p.m.	700	By S. Rly...	6-50 p.m.	Newton A. .	Exeter ¶

A Great Western Railway evacuation train schedule. It all seems very well organised, but in reality schools on their arrival at stations were put on the first train available, which was often not the train on which they were due to travel.

numbers of Bank Holiday proportions, with Wales and the West Country as favourite destinations. The Government's plans were to commence the following day, the 30th, with the evacuation of half a million London schoolchildren. In Europe, however, the Munich Agreement, handing over the Sudetenland to Hitler, was signed that day, and the evacuation scheme was called off at the last minute, much to everyone's relief, for the scheme was nothing if not rudimentary. But 4,000 children from nursery and special schools had already been evacuated by ambulances to schools and camps in the countryside – they were all back home by 6 October, but the experience gained proved indispensable for later plans.

Caroline Williams was at teacher training college in London at this time:

In September I returned to St Gabriel's College in Camberwell. Immediately we were overwhelmed by the Munich Crisis and our principal decided to send us home but asked if any of us would volunteer to act as escorts to a nursery school in the Mile End Road, before we finally went home. With two other students I started off from the Nursery in a coach with the Nursery staff, and the children, plus potties – destination unknown.

We eventually arrived in Aylesbury, Bucks. It must have been on the green of a housing estate where we were finally unloaded from the coach. The local mothers stood around and began to choose the children, 'I'll have that one', 'I'll have that one', I heard as we stood looking on. A woman asked us, 'Are you teachers?' We told her we were students and would be travelling to our homes the next morning and she hastened to offer to put us up for the night, probably relieved at the outcome.'

W.G. Eady, Deputy Under Secretary of State at the Home Office, later said that the scheme would 'just about have stood up to the requirements of getting refugees out of London and bedding them down that night while we tried to sort out what was going to happen afterwards.'

A post-mortem of the experiences of this time resulted in the responsibility for evacuation shifting in November 1938 from the Home Office to the Ministry of Health, and the Department of Health for Scotland. The recommendations of the Anderson Committee were published and led to strong pressure on the government to accept them in full. This was done, and the lessons learnt during the Munich Crisis were also incorporated – from now on the arrangement of sufficient billets in advance became a vital part of the scheme.

A new scheme was drawn up by the Ministry assisted by officers seconded by the Board of Education. This scheme divided all parts of the country into three classes: evacuation, reception and neutral areas. The evacuation areas were those from which 'priority' groups were to be given the opportunity to transfer to safer areas in the event of an emergency; reception areas were those places that would receive them; and neutral areas, as their name implied, were neither one nor the other.

Evacuation was to apply to four main groups:

1) Nearly 4,000,000 children, mothers and invalids living in cities whom the government had arranged to remove, if they wished, to safer areas.
2) Individuals who chose to leave under their own arrangements – this was known as private evacuation.
3) Business firms and private companies, known as business evacuation.
4) The government, ministers, MPs and civil servants. The Ministry of Health was to be in overall charge of the scheme, while the coordination of the Ministry's scheme was the responsibility of local education departments.

A government leaflet, Evacuation – Why and How?, issued to all households in July 1939, setting out the details of the government's evacuation scheme.

In July 1939 the Lord Privy Seal's Office issued a series of leaflets on Civil Defence which were delivered to every house in the country. The third of these, entitled Evacuation – Why

MOTHERS
Send them out
of London

ive them a chance of greater safety and healt

An evacuation poster. Once it was decided that evacuation would be voluntary, it was necessary to convince the public to cooperate. One common tactic was to appeal to mothers.

and How?, contained the following list of the evacuation areas under the government scheme:

a) London, as well as the County Boroughs of West Ham and East Ham; the Boroughs of Walthamstow, Leyton, Ilford and Barking in Essex; the Boroughs of Tottenham, Hornsey, Willesden, Acton, and Edmonton in Middlesex; b) The Medway towns of Chatham, Gillingham and Rochester; c) Portsmouth, Gosport and Southampton; d) Birmingham and Smethwick; e) Liverpool, Bootle, Birkenhead and Wallasey; f) Manchester and Salford; g) Sheffield, Leeds, Bradford and Hull; h) Newcastle and Gateshead; i) Edinburgh, Rosyth, Glasgow, Clydebank and Dundee.

The choice of evacuation areas caused many protests. For example, Croydon was originally designated a neutral area. A deputation visited the Ministry, pointing out its vulnerable position, and in July the Ministry accepted Croydon's arguments and it was redesignated. Plymouth, on the other hand, was subject to several heavy raids yet, despite many official requests, the Ministry refused to make it an evacuation area until after the heaviest raids in March and April 1941. H.P. Twyford in his book about Plymouth during the war, *It Came to Our Door*, commented: 'I do not think Plymouth ever quite forgot or forgave that disregard of their appeal to send the children away.' There was, of course, a fair amount of private evacuations made, but many parents, especially the poorer ones, were unable to arrange or afford to do so.

Early in January 1939, the government had passed on to the local authorities in the likely reception areas the details of their evacuation scheme. They asked the authorities to find out: 1) the amount of surplus accommodation on the basis of one person per habitable room; 2) the amount of this surplus to be found in houses that were suitable for reception; 3) the amount to be found in houses where the householder was willing to receive unaccompanied children, or teachers. The census established that there was enough surplus accommodation for 4,800,000 people. At the same time the Ministry carried out a survey to find out how many pregnant priority cases could be billeted in the various reception areas.

In February an ARP Department circular stated that the role of the WVS had been widened to include helping local authorities make their evacuation plans. The Ministry then assigned a reception area to each evacuation area, thus the various parts of Greater London covered by the scheme, called the Metropolitan Evacuation Area, were assigned an area roughly corresponding to that part of

A poster appealing for female volunteers to work as helpers in the evacuation service. (HMSO)

England south of a line from the Bristol Channel to the Wash. As part of the evacuation scheme, plans were made in some reception areas for communal feeding, the purpose being to save householders the responsibility of providing a mid-day meal for their evacuees. As with many pre-war preparations, such as the formation of the ARP services, responses from local authorities varied. Some, like Lingfield in Surrey, threw themselves wholeheartedly into the task, setting up reception committees and formulating detailed schemes. The response of others was, at best, lukewarm.

By the end of March the original plans for the evacuation of the Metropolitan Area had been modified to produce Plan II, and letters were sent to all schools setting out the new arrangements. These new plans covered the transport of parties from assembly points to 'entraining stations' (the railway stations from which they would catch their main train), and from these to the reception areas. They also covered the control of parties, to be carried out by 20,000 teachers and a similar number of voluntary helpers, all under the direction of twelve divisional dispersals officers. Children from handicapped, special and nursery

Evacuation rehearsal at Barnsole Road School, Gillingham, August 1939. Notice the placard bearing the school number, obviously using a similar scheme to that used in London. (Kent Messenger Newspaper Group)

The original caption for this photograph reads 'Mrs Claypole of 79 Skinner Street Chatham preparing the kits of her three youngest children before they were evacuated to a reception area'. (Kent Messenger Newspaper Group)

schools were to be moved in school parties, and housed as complete units – this applied to privately run institutions as well as state establishments. By June suitable premises had been found for 300 such parties, and by July travel arrangements for these 'special parties', as they were called, were finalised.

By May, mothers and children in the evacuation areas who wished to be included in a future evacuation had registered and were given preliminary instructions. Mothers of children under five could choose to withdraw older children from their school arrangements so that they might accompany them. Of the 245,000 estimated children under five in London, 105,000 (44 per cent) and 83,000 mothers registered for evacuation. Registration of expectant mothers took place in maternity and child welfare centres, while registration of the blind was carried out by Home Visitors.

In June 5,000 children took part in an evacuation rehearsal held in Chelsea. During the rehearsal, which lasted 1½ hours, the children assembled and were marched or bussed to their entraining stations. In Birmingham, nine schools took part in an evacuation rehearsal on 20 July, followed by a second, larger rehearsal on 28 August. June Cohen took part in another practice in Stoke Newington: 'A little while before war broke out we had a sort of practice going to the school with our suitcase and gas mask and getting on the tram to go to the railway station.' Margaret Cronin, from the Elephant & Castle, remembers some of the problems: 'As the war approached we had a series of evacuation drills, and the Headmistress sent home a list of things which we had to take with us pinned up in a blanket – we didn't have all the things.'

The log book of Stillness Road LCC (London County Council) School in Lewisham for 26 July 1939 reads:

School closes for summer holidays. All plans for evacuation are complete. Should evacuation be ordered during the holiday it would appear that the estimated school numbers would be greatly depleted as so many children expect to be out of London on holiday.

THREE

The First Evacuation

'War Task Number 1'

At the time of the Munich Crisis, Hitler had said, 'I have assured Mr Chamberlain and I emphasise it now that when this problem is solved Germany has no more territorial problems in Europe . . . I shall not be interested in the Czech State any more.' Hopes that he would keep his word, and that peace would prevail, increased through the winter but were shattered on 15 March 1939 when German forces marched into the now defenceless Czechoslovakia.

World-wide indignation followed, and what little credibility Hitler had retained was gone. The focus of European concern moved to Danzig. In the Versailles Treaty, Poland had been allocated some of what had been Prussia, in a 'corridor' allowing it access to the Baltic. Inside this corridor was the Free City of Danzig, protected by the League of Nations. A branch of the Nazi party had been set up there in 1934, and it proved very active; by the end of 1937, Danzig was completely in the hands of the Nazis, who demanded an end to League control. Germany now began a violent campaign against Poland for the return of the 'Polish Corridor'. Britain and France offered guarantees to Poland; throughout summer '39 tension mounted, until on 23 August Germany signed a non-aggression pact with Russia – and the immediate obstacle to a German invasion of Poland was removed.

A Ministry of Health notice broadcast on 24 August notified teachers in evacuation areas that it was 'considered desirable that they should return to their districts immediately' (it was, of course, still the summer holidays). While being reassured that this did not mean that evacuation would take place, the teachers were directed to report to their schools on the morning of the 26th. (At this time, the Ministry warned local authorities that they could not expect to receive more than twelve hours' notice of the initiation of the evacuation plan.) It was not only teachers who were called back early. Lillian Clegg, a housemaid in a girls' boarding school in Liverpool, remembers:

> When term ended I went as usual to my aunt's in Douglas, Isle of Man, to help in her boarding house, then I got a telegram; 'Return to work at once'. On the Thursday (31 August) we were all sent to Yeaton Pevery, near Shrewsbury. We were joined by the domestic staff from Birkenhead High School, to prepare for children to arrive on the Sunday. More jolly hard work, lots of problems, but we got a smashing school going.

Smiling evacuees, their teachers and helpers, aided by a WPC, leave London in September 1939. (London Metropolitan Archives)

In most evacuation areas, schoolchildren were called back to school on Monday 28 August to take part in a huge evacuation rehearsal. Teachers, inspectors, and helpers were on duty as children began to arrive at 6 a.m., carrying their gas masks and bags containing clothes and food. Each school was given a number and the location of their embarkation point, either for trains, buses, tubes, coaches and even private cars or river steamers. The teachers checked on the children's kit while marshals checked arrangements at the embarkation points. Miriam McLeod from Clapton took part in the practice:

> I was first evacuated at the beginning of September 1939 with my older sister's school; Clapton Girls' Secondary School. A few weeks before we had had to go for a practice evacuation; we had to go to the school with our bags and gas masks, and with our labels pinned on us; we seemed to march round a lot.

Some children went early. Betty Goodyear of Birmingham was one:

> I was evacuated with City Road Senior Girls' School about a fortnight before war was declared. Along with my sister who was 5 years younger than I, and a great many more children, all with a label tied on our coats and a packet of sandwiches, etc.
>
> As a city girl I found it very exciting to play in the local mountains among all the ferns, or paddle and fish in the river which was also very close. We had been told in school before we went that they were taking us all for two or three weeks

holiday in Wales and that if there was a war we might have to stay there. None of us dreamed that there *would* be a war and when we found we didn't go home again after weeks and weeks, and the novelty all began to wear off, I think most of them came back to Birmingham.

On 29 August Hitler demanded that Poland send a representative to Berlin, with the authority to agree to any demands put to him. It was an outrageous demand, and Poland refused. As the situation grew ever more serious the Government were faced with a quandary; it was generally expected at the time that bombing would begin immediately upon the outbreak of war, if not before, as happened with the Americans at Pearl Harbor. Thus evacuation needed to be carried out before hostilities commenced, yet at the same time such an action could be seen as provocative at a time when peace hung in the balance; there were also some in government circles who felt that evacuation might cause panic among the populace. At the very least, to put into action such an immense operation, involving 4 million

Schoolgirls (and dollies) being evacuated from Gillingham, June 1940. (Kent Messenger Newspaper Group)

people, would be hugely expensive and disruptive if, as had happened just a year before, peace could be pulled out of the hat at the last minute. Not normally associated with decisive action, Neville Chamberlain's government hesitated about giving the order that would start evacuation. On 29 August the parliamentary opposition pressed strongly for the order to be given, and a deputation to the Prime Minister from the National Council of Labour that afternoon repeated the call. But the government held out for two more days, until the morning of the 31st, when orders were finally given for the exodus to begin the next day. The government still tried desperately to assure everyone that this did not necessarily mean war; the Ministry of Health issued the following statement:

It has been decided to start evacuation of the schoolchildren and other priority classes as already arranged under the Government's scheme tomorrow, Friday, September 1. No one should conclude that this decision means that war is now regarded as inevitable.

Evacuation, which will take several days to complete, is being undertaken as a precautionary measure in view of the prolongation of the period of tension.

The Government is fully assured that the attitude of quiet confidence which the public have been displaying will continue, that no unnecessary movements

Boys of Brockley Central School, South London, assembling at the school prior to evacuation. The tall, bare-headed boy just right of centre is Doug Ryall (looking very fed-up), next to him (centre) is his younger brother, John, who like the two small children on the left, is being evacuated with his older brother's school.

Brockley Central School boys set off towards Brockley station, 2 September 1939. Notice the boys in a 'crocodile' procession on the pavement and the parents walking in the road.

which would interfere with the smooth operation of the transport arrangements will take place, and that all concerned in the receiving areas will entirely put aside every consideration of personal interest and convenience and do everything possible to contribute to the success of a great national undertaking.

That night Germany issued her demands to Poland, and without waiting for a reply ordered her armies to attack – on the following morning both the armed forces of Germany and the children of Britain's cities were on the move.

A leaflet, *War Emergency Information & Instructions* was issued containing the following information:

If you live in one of these [evacuation] areas and have a child or children of school age who you wish to be evacuated you should send them to school on the day which will be notified to you. Each child should have a handbag or case containing the child's gas mask, a change of underclothing, night clothes, house shoes or plimsolls, spare stockings or socks, a toothbrush, a comb, towel, soap and face cloth, handkerchiefs; and, if possible, a warm coat or mackintosh. Each child should bring a packet of food for the day. School children will be taken by their teachers to homes in safer districts where they will be housed by people who have already offered to receive them and look after them. Parents of school children living in these areas are strongly urged to let their children go. Parents will be told where the children are as soon as they reach their new homes. The cost of the journey will be paid by the Government.

Posters will be exhibited at the schools showing the times when mothers with children below school age should assemble at the schools, unless they have been notified in some other way. Mothers and other persons in charge of children below school age should take hand-luggage with the same equipment for themselves and their children as for school children. The names of the children should be written on a label or strong paper and sewn on to their clothes.

GOVERNMENT EVACUATION SCHEME

The Government have ordered evacuation of school children.

If your children are registered for evacuation send them to their assembly point at once.

If your children are not registered and you wish them to be evacuated, the teachers or the school keeper will help you.

If you do not wish your children to be evacuated you must not send them to school until further notice.

Posters notifying the arrival of parties in the country will be displayed at the schools at which the children assembled for evacuation.

The County Hall. S.E.1

E. M. RICH. Education Officer, L.C.C

An LCC 'Government Evacuation Scheme' poster advising parents of the commencement of evacuation.

Most important to the children was that, usually, they were allowed to take just one toy. Betty Collas remembers: 'We could take one suitcase each. I had just had my seventh birthday and I had to leave all my presents behind – we were allowed to take one toy each.' The planned medical inspection

Evacuees carry their sacks on their way to the railway station. Notice the plimsolls – many children arrived in the countryside in such unsuitable footwear.

before the children left did not take place because it was the school holidays; this was the reason why some children arrived at the reception areas with such conditions as head lice.

Within fourteen hours of the evacuation order being given, the WVS had alerted 120,000 women throughout the country, 17,000 of whom worked as escorts for the evacuees, to commence 'War task number one'. Also involved with supervision and coordination were teachers, borough officials, railway companies' and other transport workers as well as a number of voluntary helpers. Midwives were allocated to each coach or party that included expectant mothers, and a sighted guide accompanied each blind evacuee where necessary. The Police planned their routes, in London, for instance, this entailed journeys from the 1,589 assembly points to 168 entraining stations. When the actual trek began, police helped to shepherd the moving flocks with the aid of loudspeaker vans. It was the sheer scale of the thing that made it such a remarkable event and led to its nickname, 'the Great Trek'. Walter Elliott, the Minister of Health, described the exercise as 'an exodus bigger than that of Moses. It is the movement of ten armies, each of which is as big as the whole Expeditionary Force.' In London, 1.8 million potential evacuees were to go, spread over four days.

On the same day, 1 September 1939, the Railway Executive Committee was brought into being under Defence Regulations. These were pre-nationalisation times and, as today, Britain's railways were controlled by a number of railway companies. The fast-approaching war meant that the vital work of the railways and London Transport had to be coordinated; this was the purpose of the committee and its first test was to be evacuation.

The London Underground ferried many out of central London. Evacuees were entrained from seventy-two stations to outer London areas where they joined trains or boarded buses. Trains ran from the main stations from 8.30 to

A teacher's evacuation armband – LCC 0392 (Christ Church School). London elementary schools had a three- or four-figure number, non-local authority controlled elementaries like Christ Church began with a 0; special schools with an S; nurseries SN; aided, maintained and other secondaries H; and technical institutes and schools of art T. This one is a very well-made example with embroidered lettering; often they were printed or hand painted.

5.30 at nine-minute intervals with the groups' arrivals at stations timed so that the children would have less than 15 minutes to wait. Buses, single and double-decker, were also used; some London Transport buses were on the road for up to two days – a great deal of pre-planning had to be done to ensure that the double-deckers did not come across any low bridges. Other transport was also used. Betty Jones recalls:

I was almost ten when I was evacuated with my school, Manorway School, on September 2nd 1939. We were put on a bus to the Tilbury Riverside Station, where we embarked on a Thames pleasure steamer. It was a cold grey day, I remember being on deck, sitting on my case, sniffing a lemon – Mum had said this stopped you feeling sick. After a trip of about four to five hours, we landed at Yarmouth.

Metropolitan Police WPC with young evacuees, September 1939. (HMSO)

Nita Jenkins recalls that: 'We were evacuated on the pleasure steamer *Royal Daffodil* from Gravesend in Kent. My mother said her nerves were frayed as she was told there was a submarine in the area. We were taken to a Racecourse in Norfolk. During the night, in all the hysteria, someone shouted "Gas"; the blankets were taken off our beds, soaked in the horse troughs and hung over the stable doors.'

Children were ferried to their points of departure either by special train or by road transport; nearly 6,000 passenger vehicles carried over 345,000 people to the stations. As the main termini could not deal with them all, suburban stations were also used. On the Southern Railway these were New Cross Gate, Wimbledon and Richmond. On the Great Western, 50,000 children passed through Ealing Broadway Station on the first day alone. *The Unbeaten Track* described the scene:

Inside an evacuation train – a bit squashed perhaps, but not too bad. (HMSO)

. . . children [were] collected from every nook and cranny of London . . . and they poured out of the underground trains in a never-ending stream to change onto the West of England Expresses. All day they passed in a continuous stream over the foot-bridge on to the Main Line platform. Nurses were waiting there for them, and gave hot milk and tea to some who had been up and about since half-past five that morning. All the long day through there came by way of loud-speakers calm voices giving counsel and advice . . . and these voices never tired. The station rang with such admonitions as 'Hullo, children! Please take your seats quickly. The train leaves in a few minutes. Don't play with the doors and windows if you don't mind. Thank you.'

As each underground train drew in to the platforms, voluntary helpers and teachers hurried the children in crocodile formation to their point of departure . . . and at the head of many a contingent strode a boy proudly carrying a banner, not with a strange device, but with the name of his school written across it.

I saw children carrying buckets and spades . . . and I heard many a mother telling her child that he, or she, was going to have a lovely time at the seaside building castles in the sand. I took note of beaming but exhausted-looking police officers striding backwards and forwards with their arms full of very tiny tots.

As each train left Ealing Broadway or Paddington, a telegram was sent to the station master at its point of arrival, who would contact the local reception officer and transport managers so that preparations for reception of the evacuees could be initiated.

'Goodbye Hitler' – a London Transport evacuation bus. (HMSO)

Local decisions meant that some families were split up. Betty Jones remembers: 'My sister was older than me, she went to the grammar school, so we were split up.' Iris Gent said: 'I was at Roan School in Greenwich. My younger brother had just started, but the boys and girls were evacuated separately', and Eddie Roland recalls that: 'At Weymouth station for some reason, the boys and girls were segregated. As we boys were put on the train, I could see the girls walking away from me and I was frantic with worry. The last thing our Mum had said was "stay together". I was desperately trying to see which way they were going – but I couldn't.'

In London 300 special parties, comprising a total of 9,500 children, went on the first day; 3,823 expectant mothers and 2,068 blind people went on the second. London's expectant mothers were sent to Oxford, Cambridge, Northampton, Bury St Edmunds, Eastbourne and Trowbridge, and most of the blind were sent to Luton. Green Line coaches were quickly converted to ambulances, each carrying eight or ten stretcher cases, to remove many of the capital's hospital patients in preparation for the expected air raid casualties.

Outside London, events moved equally quickly. On 1 September, 40,000 were moved

Evacuees being shepherded on to their train. (HMSO)

Green Line coaches converted to ambulances. (HMSO)

Evacuees and troops at the railway station. (HMSO)

from Leeds in under seven hours, and Glasgow and Edinburgh stations were busy until the evening. Over the 1st and the 2nd, 37,000 people from Rochester, Chatham, Gillingham and Rainham were moved to other parts of Kent; 30,000 from Southampton and Gosport to Hampshire, Dorset and Wiltshire; and 22,000 from Birmingham to stations in the Severn Valley, Worcestershire, Gloucestershire, Shropshire, Warwickshire and Monmouthshire. Evacuees from South Shields and Sunderland reported to receive instructions on the 2nd, and those from Jarrow, Hebburn, Hartlepool and Middlesborough a day later. Between the 1st and the 5th, 36,000 evacuees were taken from Liverpool and Birkenhead, and on the 5th, 2,600 from the neighbourhood of Belvedere and Erith went to parts of Kent. Over 6,000 were taken from Middlesborough to Scarborough. Not all the evacuations were completed before war was declared. Unaccompanied children from Tynemouth and Wallsend were evacuated on the 6th, and mothers with children on the 7th.

This first part of the evacuation process was generally considered a huge success. To quote from *Ourselves in Wartime*: 'Transport did not break down; no children were lost; no one was injured; families and parties did not get broken up on the journey. The fear that transport might collapse under the strain was completely unfounded.' It is even more remarkable when it is remembered that while this great exodus was taking place, ordinary peacetime life was still carrying on – commuters still travelled, and the rush hour still happened. The evacuation trains had to be slotted in between the regular services, which explains why so many of them took so long. However, such a great undertaking did not pass off completely without incident, although most of the hitches were fairly minor. David Wood from Kentish Town describes one such journey:

> I was evacuated in early September 1939. We assembled at the school in the morning, and from there we were all bussed to Paddington station, where there was a special train. For some reason the locomotive was taken off at Swindon, so the trip took six hours instead of the normal hour and a half – there was no corridor and I can vividly remember the boys peeing out of the window. We finally arrived at Bristol Temple Meads station – we had to wait for ages. In the end our teacher had a row with the Billeting Officer. We were eventually taken to Falfield. When we got there the Billeting Officer had gone home – he must have thought we weren't coming, I suppose, so that night we slept on the floor of the village hall.

A father says farewell to his daughter, Croydon, 1939.

Long journeys were often a part of the process. Doreen Last was evacuated from Colchester in 1940: 'We left very quickly and travelled all day. At 7 p.m. the train stopped and our neighbour shouted out of the window to a linesman as to our whereabouts; we were at Hitchen, Herts, a one hour journey from Colchester! Thus we continued until 11 p.m.' Eddie Roland was reminded that: 'I was put into a carriage with other boys and a teacher, Mr Pearson, from our school. We had nothing to eat or drink for the trip, but Mr Pearson shared his cheese sandwiches with us. We finally left Weymouth at 6 p.m. Everyone was exhausted with tiredness and worry and I fell asleep with my head leaning against the window.'

It was soon realised that the numbers turning up for evacuation were considerably less than had registered, so the task could be telescoped, the London operation taking three days instead of the planned four. Of the 1.8 million potential London evacuees, 660,000 (36 per cent) actually went, comprising 377,000 children accompanied by their teachers, 275,000 mothers and children, 3,500 expectant mothers and a similar number of blind adults. In the provinces, the figures were 1.2 million of a possible 3.6 million (33 per cent), 758,000 children accompanied by their teachers, 445,000 mothers and children, 11,300 expectant mothers, 5,300 blind adults, and 872 'cripples'. In all, about half the eligible children from London, 40 per cent from Glasgow (close to the overall Scottish average of 37 per cent), 25 per cent from Birmingham and Coventry, with Sheffield as low as 15 per cent. In the second week in September, registration for a further wave of evacuation was encouraged, but the response was very limited. In February 1940 the Minister of Health, Walter Elliot, announced plans for the evacuation of schoolchildren in the event of serious bombing. This time the parents who registered were asked to sign an undertaking that they would send their children when ordered to do so and that they would allow them to stay in the reception areas until the school parties returned.

On the outbreak of war, a new ministry, the Ministry of Home Defence, took over responsibility for ARP matters, including coordination of evacuation, with the Board of Education taking responsibility for the billeting of evacuated children.

The evacuation scheme had been the first task for the WVS, and was the start of a long tradition of service to the public for the women in green. Joyce Fry remembers how: 'A lady in a green uniform and large hat leaned in the window and gave us all a little packet of nuts and raisins and an orange. I immediately poked my finger into the orange, sucked out all the juice and discarded the rest (I did not see another orange until after the war).' Clarice Ruaux from Jersey recalls how: 'That night we were taken in coaches to this high school and an excellent meal was served by the WVS ladies. It was the first meal we'd had since Wednesday lunchtime when we'd had our dinner on the beach.' In October, Lady Reading, the founder and Chairman of the WVS, described in a broadcast to the USA the work of the WVS during the first evacuation:

> The labels to write, the knapsacks to pack, the mugs of milk to be handed out, the slices of bread and butter to be cut, the rooms and barns to be made ready

The scale of it all. (HMSO)

for the children's reception, the palliasses to be stuffed with straw – all this was the job of the women. They took the city children to the outbound trains, looked after them during the journey, and when they arrived at their destination there were the women of the little towns and villages waiting to welcome the children with hot drinks and country kindness.

These were the wives of labourers, railwaymen, cabinet ministers, farmers, parsons, all kinds of women of every political colour. Since then they have started among themselves canteens where the children can get a good mid-day dinner near their school, and where, at the weekend, their visiting parents can also be fed. They have strengthened the local health services with voluntary nurses, organised knitting and sewing clubs to help provide warm country clothes for the children in the coming winter months.

Just before the outbreak of war, at the end of August, Lord Woolton had made a radio appeal for blankets to be handed in to post offices whence they would be passed on to the WVS. The USA sent a large consignment of palliasse covers, which were later used as sleeping bags.

OTHER EVACUATIONS

Besides the official government scheme, there were several other types of evacuation being planned in the period before war broke out.

Private Evacuation

As has already been said, the first advice given to householders suggested that they make private arrangements with friends to receive them, or their children, or that they rent vacant property in neutral or reception areas. This reflects the almost complete lack of understanding of the lifestyle of the urban working class so often displayed by Government officials during this period. When the official scheme was developed, the earlier do-it-yourself scheme continued to be an option, becoming known as 'private evacuation'. A section in Public Information Booklet No. 3, *Evacuation – Why and How?* issued by the Lord Privy Seal's Office in July 1939, dealt with the issue of 'Private Arrangements':

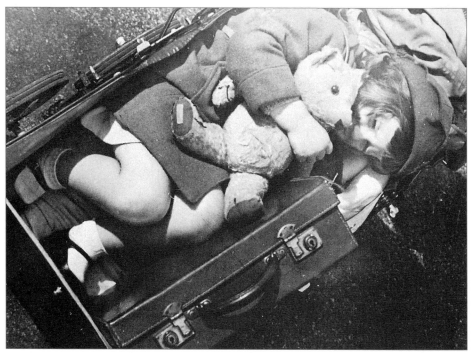

The original caption for this photograph from September 1939 reads 'A little Gillingham girl clutches her teddy in an effort to overcome homesickness'. (Kent Messenger Newspaper Group)

Children boarding a steamer in Portsmouth for evacuation to the Isle of Wight.

If you have made private arrangements for getting away your children to relatives or friends in the country, or intend to make them, you should remember that while the Government evacuation scheme is in progress ordinary railway and road services will necessarily be drastically reduced and subject to alteration at short notice. Do not, therefore, in an emergency leave your private plans to be carried out at the last minute. It may then be too late.

R.M. Titmus estimated that between June and September 1939, 2 million people were involved in private evacuation. As war approached there was a flood of private evacuees. Margaret Cronin describes conditions at one large London station: 'Mum had a sister who lived in Cranbrook in Kent and she arranged for us to go and stay with her. On Friday evening, 1st September 1939, we all went to London Bridge station, it was packed and we couldn't get a train. We stayed on the wooden benches overnight and went down early on Saturday morning on a hop-picking train.'

Much private evacuation involved staying with friends and acquaintances in the country. Tom Dewar remembers:

When war broke out I was living with my parents and younger brother in a house some two miles out of the village of Callander, in Perthshire. Immediately we were swamped by telephone requests from relations, friends (and their friends!) anxious to get away from the larger cities in fear of the air raids which were expected immediately. That evening our house contained eighteen extra people; we had only five bedrooms, so all rooms except the kitchen were used; my brother and I had to sleep on the billiard table, much to our chagrin.

Doreen Hooper lived with her mother in a small cottage in Teignmouth: 'Mrs Gernell from Chingford was a great friend so mother invited her two daughters and their children to stay. We moved next door and lived with Mum's sister so that the two families could live in our house.' Ursula Nott, from Pebmarsh in Essex, recalls: 'In 1940 I had my house full of friends from London', and Rita Curtis: 'Then the bombings got heavier, they used to jettison their bombs over Clacton on their way back from London. Mum decided it was getting a bit dangerous so she sent me off to stay with my grandmother – about three miles away! I used to come home at the weekend to Mum and Dad's.'

Finding suitable accommodation became the greatest single problem for the authorities organising evacuation and reception areas. When the official evacuation commenced in September a Government broadcast advised parents living in the evacuation areas that if their children were on holiday they should leave them there, where billeting allowances could be paid, if it were a reception area. But not all reception areas proved to be either willing or able to provide sufficient billets, and within those areas not all billeting officers proved to be hard-working or effective. The leaflet *War Emergency Information & Instructions*, produced at the beginning of the war, had this to say about 'private arrangements':

> If you have made private arrangements to send your children to friends or relatives, send them away immediately.
>
> Persons not engaged in work and not falling within the scope of the Government evacuation plans will not be prevented from leaving evacuable areas. While the Government evacuation scheme is in progress ordinary rail and road services will be drastically reduced. You should do nothing to impede the working of the Government plans. Otherwise you may seriously endanger a scheme intended to safeguard young persons whose lives and health are vital to the future of the nation.
>
> Persons who make their own arrangements to move from one part of the country to another should take food sufficient for one or two days with them. This is to prevent a sudden new demand being made upon local shops before steps can be taken through ordinary channels to increase their supplies.

The main evacuation was followed by supplementary evacuations throughout the winter of 1939, but of the 16,000 London schoolchildren seeking to join their school groups, over half had to wait for some months before billets could be found. To try to overcome the problem of finding appropriate billets it was agreed in June 1940 that the Government would give free travel vouchers to mothers in the evacuation areas with children under school age and to pay billeting allowance if they made their own arrangements for accommodation outside the areas of danger. This was known as the 'assisted private evacuation scheme'; it met with some success, and in October the scheme was extended to include expectant mothers, the aged, infirm, blind, invalids or homeless persons who normally lived in the Greater London Evacuation Area, and in December this was further extended to unaccompanied children. At the same time, a similar scheme was introduced covering transfer to Northern Ireland and Eire. In all, about 1¼ million people were helped in this way.

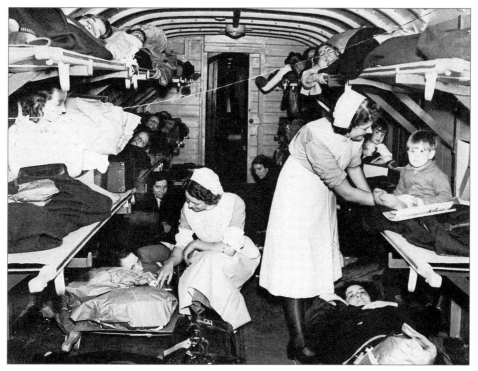

A converted railway carriage on an evacuee hospital train. (Kent Messenger Newspaper Group)

Vera Sibley was sixteen when her younger brother and sister were evacuated from Halesowen in 1941:

Handsworth is just a hop, skip and jump from Avery's at Smethwick, who were making gun carriages – my mother worked there. Lord Haw Haw kept mentioning Avery's on the radio, my mother got very afraid and as the older three children worked she paid to send them to Hagley, West Midlands, to two schoolteachers who lived in the middle of a field and kept seven cats. This came from an 'ad' in the *Birmingham Mail*.

We were worried about them as we heard such awful tales so we took it in turns to visit them and to stay the night. They were very happy and contented, and, needless to say, benefited educationally from the teachers. I remember going to this untidy but very comfortable bungalow where the atmosphere was relaxed and happy.

My mother paid about 14/- a week each, and considering that was all in it was very good value. I think the teachers regarded it as their war work.

There were inevitably gaps left in the official schemes, such as the elderly, or families of several generations who wished to stay together. Mrs R. Channing was (very) pregnant when she was evacuated from Jersey:

A group of London schoolchildren at Waterloo station in December 1939. This was part of a planned second wave of evacuees, but the response was extremely poor.

We arrived eventually at Weymouth. Expectant mothers were being sent to the Midlands, but they wanted to put my son into a home and I would not let him go. There was no bed for me anywhere, it was such a bad time, wounded soldiers from France etc. The only help I had was from the Salvation Army, They were wonderful, they gave me a bed for the night, then they sent me some distance from Weymouth where I stayed a week or so and the babies, a boy and a girl, were born.

Several voluntary organisations stepped in to fill these gaps, such as the Friends' War Victims Relief Committee. A leaflet they produced described some of the committee's work:

One of the weak spots in the evacuation scheme is the 'returns' from unhappy billets. As a practical experiment to find a remedy for this, we have invited some 'returns' to go again, this time to empty houses, in families, with shelter neighbours,

HELP US TO TAKE THEM FROM THIS—

TO THE VILLAGE PUMP.

AND THE COUNTRY LANES

A page from a Society of Friends leaflet asking for help to evacuate inner-city families.

taking their own furniture if they have any left. The country conditions they will live in have been explained to them beforehand. Thus loneliness and the shock of unexpectant environment, should be alleviated, while wardens at the reception end help them find their feet.

An option for those who could afford it, was to rent a house in the reception areas. As the war went on and previously safe areas came under threat, some who had rented houses there moved on to new safe areas, sometimes moving several times as the air assault changed its targets. This became known as 'Bomb-dodging'. Kenneth Dobson's family moved from Grays in Middlesex: 'The bombing was so bad that Dad got a job in Banbury in Oxfordshire; he was a baker. He got us a place there and mum and I went to join him.'

Evacuation of the Government

One of the aspects of evacuation looked at by the ARP Committee was 'The Movement of the Seat of Government'. Weighing the advantages of removing the Government from the dangers of air attack against the blow to the country's morale that such a move might cause, the committee decided that the decision must, of course, ultimately lay with whichever government was in power at the time, but in its first report to the government in December 1925, it recommended that the Office of Works prepare schemes for both complete and partial evacuation. Partial evacuation would either be in the event of extensive damage to

Atlas Insurance Company evacuating to Kingswood, Surrey, 26 August 1939. (Courtesy of Guardian Royal Exchange PLC)

government buildings, or as a result of the decision to move, as the ARP put it, '*les Ministères les moins utiles*', or those ministries least involved in the war effort, such as the Board of Education. Should such a move prove necessary, the ARP Committee suggested Birmingham or Liverpool as possible alternative locations.

In 1934 the committee again reported to the government on the subject. As a result of this, ministers recommended that plans should be pushed ahead for evacuation of the less essential departments, and that a scheme, already discussed, should be put into action for building underground bomb and gas-proof citadels and war-rooms around London. Eight citadels were eventually built – at Cricklewood, Curzon Street, Dollis Hill, Harrow, Horseferry Road, Horseguards, Ludgate and Whitehall.

By the outbreak of war the Office of Works had prepared detailed plans, firstly for the evacuation to the West Country of 16,000 persons involved in the administration of central government, and secondly for the evacuation of a further 44,000 departmental staff to various locations around the country. Called the 'Black Move', and the 'Yellow Move' respectively, these could be carried out at short notice over a period of three to four days. To this end, the Office of Works took over 220 hotels, 30 schools and various other buildings in the provinces. The hotels were told to clear out existing guests, often at extremely short notice, and then remain empty, at the public's expense, for weeks afterwards. Some early evacuation of departmental staff did take place involving about 20,000 civil servants. Some 1,300 employees of the Ministry of Labour were relocated to Southport and were visited there by their minister, Mr Ernest Brown. They were, on the whole, so critical about the move that he recommended that further evacuations be suspended, at least until any assault on the capital began. The main complaints were about poor accommodation and a general dissatisfaction with the disruption of the members' private and social lives. Early in 1940, in response to continued complaints, the government announced several concessions to the staff involved, including assistance in transferring their families to the reception area.

Other groups were moved to different areas: Air Ministry staff were transferred to Stroud and Stonehouse at the end of November. From the middle of September 1939, Admiralty civil servants began to arrive in Bath on special trains, to be joined by several thousand of their colleagues over the next few months. Most of the city's hotels were taken over to be used as offices, and the civil servants were billeted with families throughout the city, who were given the sum of one guinea (£1.05) a week to provide bed, breakfast and evening meal for each 'evacuee'. David Wood from Kentish Town went with the Admiralty civil servants: 'My dad worked in the Admiralty, and in 1942 they were moved to Bath, Dad rented a house and so I went back to live with them. When the Baedecker raid on Bath happened, the house was badly damaged.'

Then came the Blitzkrieg and the German attack on France, during which the seat of the French Government was moved, first from Paris to Tours, and then to Bordeaux. These moves added considerably to the confusion and muddle that characterised the fall of France, and the British Government, learning from this, abandoned the immediate plans for its own evacuation, looking instead to the citadels it had constructed. Evacuation of departmental staff continued, however,

'Billet – Eyhurst Court, Kingswood, Surrey' the alternative head office of the Atlas Insurance Company, normally based in the City of London – not all business evacuations meant roughing it. (Courtesy of Guardian Royal Exchange PLC)

and indeed was accelerated, partly so that suitable accommodation in London might be released for the rapidly expanding civil service necessary for war work.

By early June 1940 about 30,000 officials had been evacuated under the 'Yellow Move', including the staff of the Ministry of Food to North Wales. During the second half of that year and the first half of 1941, invasion was regarded as imminent on several occasions, and the plans for the complete evacuation of Government from London were held in abeyance, until such time as the capital was threatened. Under this scheme, the 'Black Move', taking one day, would come first. At six hours' notice, over 1,600 buses in convoy would transport the officials to the rendezvous point at Eton School's playing fields in Slough, from where they would be taken to Slough and Beaconsfield stations. The 'Yellow Move' would take two days, using the same routes. In an interesting echo of the children's evacuation, all persons authorised to travel were to be issued with labels as a form of ticket to board the buses. The move never went ahead as Germany turned her attention to Russia and air raids subsided.

Business Evacuation

Early in 1939 the Government declared that the decision to evacuate businesses not directly involved in war production to neutral or reception areas was for the firms themselves to decide, although it nevertheless encouraged them to make such a move before any conflict started. Responsibility for giving advice on such moves was passed to the Department of Health.

A good example of those city businesses seeking alternative accommodation pre-war was Lloyd's of London. One of their biggest problems in finding accommodation was the fact that, should they move, the marine insurance companies, the brokers, and other sections of the insurance market would need to move with them. It was estimated that of the 20,000 people employed in the market, 5,000 would need to be billeted near any alternative centre. A further complication was the need to coordinate such a move with the Government, so as not to clash with their plans for civilian evacuation. In fact, at this time, the government instructed businesses to seek relocation to neutral areas, where children would not be sent, so as to avoid such clashes. Eventually, Lloyd's leased the greater part of Pinewood Film Studios at Iver in Buckinghamshire, where they set up underwriting rooms, committee offices and so forth, among the carpenters' stores and sound stages. House-to-house canvassing found 5,000 billets in the surrounding area, and 500 staff were moved there on the weekend before war broke out, so that on 4 September the Pinewood Studios were opened as Lloyd's new premises. Other famous 'evacuees' included the Bank of England, parts of the BBC, and the London School of Economics. Iris Gent remembers life at the wartime LSE:

In 1943 I went to the London School of Economics, which had been evacuated to Cambridge, where we borrowed the lecture rooms of Peterhouse. We had a

" You should have laid more stress on the fact that we were *Business* evacuees . . ."

A David Langdon cartoon: business evacuees.

Women Fireguards outside the canteen at Pinewood Studios where Lloyd's of London evacuated in 1939. (Courtesy of Lloyd's of London)

A bus taking Lloyd's staff to their billets. (Courtesy of Lloyd's of London)

wonderful time; we had so many Jewish professors who'd come over from Europe – although sometimes their accents were a bit impenetrable. All the lectures were open – anybody could come in, there were Poles, Americans, all sorts.

Once the idea of the evacuation of the government was abandoned, so there followed a rapid slowing down of business evacuation. More and more private firms were going over to war work for the government. Its supply departments naturally wanted them to remain in close contact. Subsequently, the business exodus from London slowed to a trickle. When the London Blitz began the government did consider putting pressure on the Law Courts and certain businesses to leave London, but difficulties in finding suitable accommodation delayed any decision, and the rapid decline in raiding from the beginning of 1941 then made that decision unnecessary. There were, of course, many relocations during this period brought about by the destruction of industrial and business premises, but other than this the number of moves was small.

FOUR

'Leave Them Where They Are, Mother'

Almost from its foundation in 1925, the ARP Committee had recognised that it would be necessary to 'encourage' the general public to participate in any voluntary evacuation scheme. However, little was done until the late thirties, when developments in Europe, especially Spain, brought fresh impetus to the issue of evacuation. In his book *ARP*, J.B.S. Haldane recounts his experiences of evacuation in Spain during the civil war:

> It is very difficult to get people to evacuate Madrid, although a few shells fall on it on most days. When I was there in April 1937 there was a huge poster in the Puerta del Sol representing women and children fleeing from burning buildings, and bearing the words 'Evacuad Madrid'. It was still there in January 1938, and there were threatening notices on the walls, saying that towards the end of the month food supplies would be cut off from those who had refused to evacuate when ordered to do so. But people realise that nowhere in loyal Spain are they safe from bombing aeroplanes.

The government booklet *Evacuation – Why and How?* issued in July 1939, sought to tackle the problem:

> There are still a number of people who ask 'What is the need for all this business about evacuation? Surely if war comes it would be better for families to stick together and not go breaking up their homes?'
>
> It is quite easy to understand this feeling, because it is difficult for us in this country to realise what war in these days might mean. If we were involved in a war, our big cities might be subjected to determined attacks from the air – at any rate in the early stages – and although our defences are strong and are rapidly growing stronger, some bombers would undoubtedly get through.
>
> *Do not hesitate to register your children under this scheme, particularly if you are living in a crowded area.* Of course it means heartache to be separated from your children, but you can be quite sure that they will be well looked after. That will relieve you of one anxiety at any rate. You cannot wish, if it is possible to evacuate them, to let your children experience the dangers and fears of air attack in crowded cities.

A number of mothers in certain areas have shown reluctance to register. Naturally, they are anxious to stay by their menfolk. Possibly they are thinking that they might as well wait and see; that it may not be so bad after all. *Think this over carefully and think of your child or children in good time.* Once air attacks have begun it might be very difficult to arrange to get away.

The thrust of the campaign revolved around the then current view of a future war beginning with huge, devastating air raids, and a sense of urgency that the cities be evacuated before this began. Early posters showed women and children against a backdrop of devastation. The shock tactics had their effect; September 1939 came, the evacuees were bustled out, everyone held their breath – and nothing happened! During the autumn of 1939 the dread of bombing quickly began to recede as the weeks dragged on and the expected massed air raids failed to materialise; indeed, there were not only no massed raids, there were no raids at all!

The war was expected to be intensely violent, but short, no thought had been given to a longer, more drawn-out affair. Walter Hurst from Birkenhead recalls the general feeling that 'it would all be over in a few weeks':

'Leave the children where they are.' The authorities worked hard to convince parents not to bring their children back, but the phoney war convinced many to do just that.

'Evacuad Madrid': a poster issued by the Council for the Defence of Madrid during the Spanish Civil War.

A pre-war evacuation poster from the Ministry of Health. Notice the devastated city scene in the background. (HMSO)

I and my sister aged respectively nine and seven were evacuated with our local council school to Harlech in North Wales a few days before war was declared. We fondly imagined that we would only be away a short time but in the end it turned out to be nearly four years for me and five for my sister.

Lillian Clegg remembers feeling much the same: 'Of course, everyone was thinking that the war would soon be over and drifting back home – we came home for Christmas.'

Through that autumn and winter an almost complete lack of war activity in Western Europe meant that for Britons the biggest danger was being killed on the blacked-out roads, rather than by enemy action. Some people began to call this period the 'bore war'. Although heavy losses caused by German attacks on merchant shipping in the Atlantic led to the introduction of rationing at the start of 1940, the war on the home front was something of an anti-climax, if a welcome one. For many, the need for evacuation seemed to be over already; in the first few weeks of September there was a trickle of returning evacuees which soon became a flood; by the middle of September the Minister of Health found it necessary to advise mothers *not* to return home. The drift back by mothers was especially marked – by Christmas nearly 90 per cent of the mothers evacuated in September had returned home, compared with about 40 per cent of unaccompanied children. One mother said that her reason for returning was that she could no longer stand being unable to buy sliced bread.

The first official count in January 1940 indicated that over 900,000 evacuees had returned in all, about 60 percent, and the trend was repeated in business evacuations, though on a much smaller scale. The government were deeply concerned, their evacuation scheme, which had gone off so well, was on the verge of collapse. The Prime Minister, in a speech at Mansion House, emphasised that the danger was far from over. The flow of returnees did slacken, but it was probably going to do so anyway; Christmas was a crucial time when the pain of family separation had been at its height, and those who had been able to resist the temptation to bring their children home at that point were likely to be strong enough to resist further.

On 15 February the Ministry of Health issued a circular stating that the Government proposed to continue with a scheme of voluntary evacuation, but that it would in future be confined to schoolchildren and would only come into

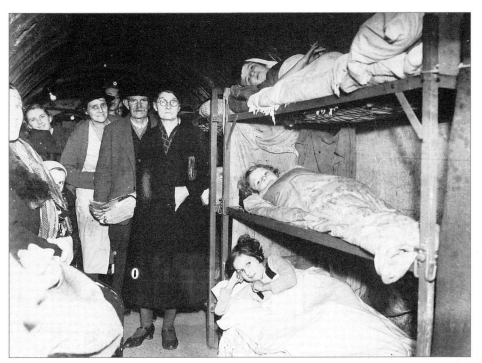

Those who stayed behind: residents seek refuge in a makeshift public shelter. (Kent Messenger Newspaper Group)

operation once serious attacks had developed. Some of the school buildings taken over by the ARP after the first evacuation for use as depots had to be handed back as the drift of returnees increased. Now another problem emerged; many of the teachers were still in the reception areas. Linda Stebbing was a teacher from Woodford:

> Teachers were 'called up' and were sent wherever needed. I was sent to Dagenham, where the schools were full of pupils whose parents brought them back from their safe havens thinking as all seemed quiet – it was the 'phoney war' – but not for long! The Dagenham teachers were still evacuated and couldn't return until ordered to do so.

The start of the Blitzkrieg posed further problems; many of the first reception areas came under invasion threat, while the cities were left in peace. Then when bombing did start in May, the targets were often coastal or provincial towns; often the evacuees seemed in more danger in their billets than at home. Betty Jones describes what happened at her first billet:

> We stayed there until the summer when there was an air raid on Norwich, the lady said she wasn't going to stay there, and went to live with her sister in the

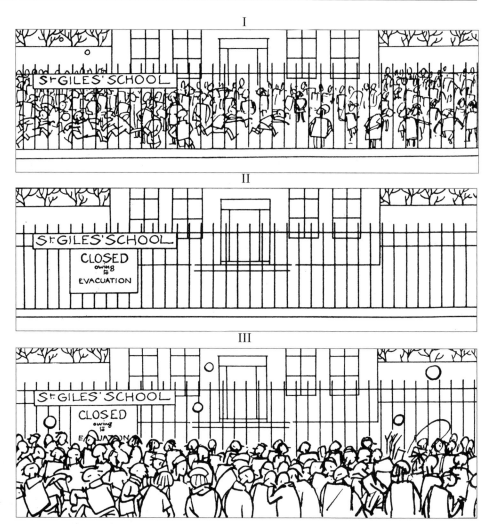

A Fougasse cartoon – 'the changing face of Britain'. Primary Education I: Pre-evacuation – the playground is full of children. II. Evacuation – an empty playground. III. Soon after – the school is still closed but the children have returned.

Midlands. Mum said 'You're getting raids and we're not – you might as well come home.' I got back just as the blitz started.

It is easy to understand how, when the feared raids failed to materialise, so many parents wanted their children back. The belief that massed raids would start immediately was so strong that their non-appearance was generally seen not as a breathing space, but as a sign that they would not happen at all. With hindsight we can see now how wrong an assumption that was, but it is easy to understand why people thought that way. What is far harder to understand is why, once the raids did start in 1940, parents still refused to send their children away, or even worse, brought them back. In his book, *The Lesson of London*, Ritchie Calder approaches the question:

> Many people blame the mothers who did not go, or who failed to send their children out, or who, having gone or sent the children, abandoned evacuation. That was a mistake, of course, but I cannot take the 'they-deserve-what-they-get' line, because I know the powerful family ties which were partly responsible. Women wanted to be in their homes and to care for the working members of the family; they clung to family unity with a devotion which is not to be lightly condemned. Life has little meaning in the drabness of working-class life except in terms of flesh-and-blood relationships. Remarkable and often tragic was the way families said at the heart of the Blitz, 'better we all die together'.

Rita Curtis recalls that: 'My school was evacuated but I didn't go, I was my mum's "little precious gem", or my dad's. She wouldn't send me away.'

Sometimes life in the country was just too different – Ursula Nott commented: 'Unfortunately they couldn't stand the quietness, and they missed the social side of sheltering in the Underground so in the end they left to go back to London and the noise of gunfire and bombs.' Brian Martin's parents had an evacuee family from Bethnal Green at their farm near Newmarket: 'One day they came to say goodbye on their way back to London. As they said, "We'd rather face the bleedin' bombs than live in the country." Looking back it must have been hard for people to go from a town life to an isolated country life.' Sometimes homesickness was too much, as Lavender Clarke remembers: 'There were two sisters and a brother, Evelyn, Barbara, and Ben Phelps, and another boy, he was the most homesick, being on his own. They were all dreadfully homesick, they used to cry and mother used to comfort them.' Sometimes the billet, or the foster parents were unbearable, a situation experienced by Iris Gent: 'Then I went to Ninfield Manor House with three or four other girls. The family lived at one end of the house – we weren't allowed to go through the baize door, we lived in the kitchens! One of the other girls and I decided to run away; it took quite a while to save up the bus fare. When I got home, my Mother already knew – they'd sent a telegram. I was sent back after a couple of days.' Sometimes the parents couldn't stand being parted from their children. Mary Spink has memories of this: 'They were only with us for three months, then their mother came and took them back; it must have been so hard on the parents to put their children on a train and then not see them for

For those who remained through the Blitz, life revolved around the shelters, or the Underground. (HMSO)

months.' There were almost as many reasons as there were evacuees, as Doreen Last recalls: 'Once a month Father and our neighbour's husband travelled up together to visit us, quite terrified of the blitz, we later learned, to the extent that by Christmas they both signed forms to end our evacuation and took us home.'

Tom Dewar from Callander, Perthshire, remembers:

> It was, I think, on the 11th September when our new 'guests' arrived. They were all boys, two pairs of brothers and one other. All came from the Possilpark district of Glasgow. The next morning my mother found to her horror that the beds were all 'wet', and that all the children had heads infested with lice. We still had two maidservants who lived in a house nearby and came in daily. They and my mother gave the boys baths (they were filthy) and treated their heads, despite tremendous objections and tears. Some clothing was discarded, and items taken from my brothers' and my wardrobes to replace them. The children were never happy. They missed the excitement of Glasgow life. They hated – and were scared of – sleeping in bedrooms on their own, even though lights were left on. They were quickly bored. The food did not suit, although they ate with us and had the same meals. There were cows in the fields adjoining our house; they were scared of these. Their parents arrived from Glasgow on a visit about ten days later, met by my mother at the station. One of the evacuees mothers was annoyed – abusive – because of the removal and burning of the garments, despite the replacement by my brother's shirt, shorts and jacket. None seemed to be grateful. On their next visit the parents stated that they were taking the boys back home as they didn't like the way they were being treated.

One of the most difficult hurdles to overcome was the lack of understanding, caused by huge differences in attitudes and experiences, between those who were responsible for organising the evacuation schemes, and those who were the subject of the schemes. The organisers were high-ranking civil servants, at that time all of them male, and from upper middle-class backgrounds. As such, they would have been sent away to boarding school at a very early age, and, if they now had children, they would have little to do with them, this being the job of women, and mostly servants at that. However, their 'clients' were mostly women and children from the inner-city working classes, who had little in life except 'the family', an extended group whose bonds were extremely tight and whose instinct was to come together in times of trouble. Trying to convince such families to do the complete opposite required a knowledge and understanding of their lifestyle and their values, hardly prevalent among the middle classes at the time, and an immense amount of tact and patience. Despite the odds, in some cases this is exactly what was achieved; in London the Ministry of Health tried to cut down the number of children remaining by sending visitors out to their families, mainly people known to them, to try to change their minds. By this means, the numbers remaining in the capital were cut by one third.

The authorities tried to discourage children from returning home, even for short periods. The greatest temptation came during school holidays, so the Board of Education asked Local Education Authorities in the receiving areas to keep school buildings and playgrounds open during the holidays, so that children might be kept occupied 'without additional demands being made on the goodwill of their hosts in billets'. In order to facilitate this, teachers' holidays were arranged on a rota system. As a further discouragement, parents were warned that, should their children go home for the school holidays, 'billets may not be available to them on their return'. The LCC introduced the cheap visits scheme which enabled parents to visit their evacuated children at reduced rates, on production of a voucher from their Education Authority. Tickets were for one or three days, and there was a special eight-day ticket for the summer. The evacuees and their families eagerly looked forward to these visits – Anne Peppercorn remembers: 'Dad used to come and visit me by train, Mum was ill. The journey took ten to twelve hours and he had to stand all the way. He came every month none the less.' – but the visits could cause problems for the billeters as Evelyn Baker explains: 'We got another family, the Hardings, from Stratford. There was Mrs Harding and Lynette. Mr Harding ran a garage, so he had petrol. He used to drive down and bring some relatives – we used to have a houseful!'

HASTINGS GRAMMAR SCHOOL.

At: St. Albans School,
ST. ALBANS.

July, 1941.

Dear Sir (Madam),

Summer Recess, 1941.

It is proposed that the present term shall end at midday on Saturday, July 26th, and the new term begin at 9.30 a.m. on Monday, August 25th. Between these dates organised recreational activity will be available in St. Albans. The following important points are brought to the notice of Parents.

1. The return of boys to Hastings is strongly deprecated by the Authorities.

2. There is no obligation on the part of a Foster-parent to keep a billet open when it is left vacant for more than one week. It is also pointed out that a sudden emergency in another part of the country may result in vacant billets here being utilised for other purposes.

3. The Billeting Authority is unwilling to rebillet boys whose billets are lost by contravention of paragraph 2.

I would, therefore, strongly urge upon parents the wisdom of leaving their boys in St. Albans during the recess, or of negotiating the date and period of absence with Foster Parents, so that no difficulty will arise. In this latter connection I would draw attention to the terms of the form to be completed below, and to request that it be not returned to me until the latter section has been complied with.

Yours faithfully,

SGD. M. G. G. HYDER.

Headmaster.

A letter from the head of Hastings Grammar School, July 1941, discouraging the return home of the boys during the summer recess.

Iris Miller from Westminster remembers her foster mother:

Mrs Henry was very kind to us. In her beautiful garden she had a large comfortable summerhouse known as 'the dugout', and there she would accommodate our family when they needed a respite from the war. In September my mum and dad were invited to stay for the week. We had a wonderful holiday with marvellous weather; it is a memory I treasure because I didn't see my father again as he died the following April. After he died my mother came down to Holcombe to live with me and Mrs Henry.

Many lessons were taken on board after the problems of the first evacuation. The book *Ourselves in Wartime* describes some of the measures introduced at the time of the second evacuation:

Arrangements were made for the entertainment of evacuees, particularly young mothers, who had suffered such discomfort in their billets during the first evacuation. Hostels were opened for them, where they could lead a communal life, and look after their own young children; the policy became to billet unaccompanied children with small households, and the mothers and children with them, going to the hostels. Provision was made for entertainment clubs for mothers, and nursery centres for working mothers; communal meals and laundries solved many problems, and week-end hostels were set up where husbands could stay on a visit.

It had been thought that billeting evacuees as near their homes was best, but the drawback of this policy soon became obvious – Caroline Williams recalls how: 'Later, Newport was designated an evacuation area and an evacuation plan was put into operation. We had to lose a teacher from my school to go with the evacuees but nobody wanted to go to the reception area, which turned out to be further up the valleys into the coal-mining towns. Apparently, a number of the children walked back home after the first night; after all, what was eight miles down the valley road to Newport?'

A Ministry of Health leaflet for billeting officers dated August 1941 addressed the issue of returning evacuees:

Billeting officers and welfare workers should of course do everything in their power to discourage a drift back to evacuation areas, and, if they find that evacuated persons are uncomfortable in their billets and likely to leave them, they should take all possible steps to remove the difficulties and find new billets, irrespective of whether the persons concerned arrived in the district as part of an organised party or were billeted as a result of private arrangements. If the mothers themselves insist on returning home everything possible should be done to influence them to leave the children in the receiving area – they can of course, be . . . billeted as unaccompanied children. Care should be taken to see that any children under 5 years of age are left with a willing householder, or otherwise suitably provided for, and not compulsorily billeted.

Sometimes when families were spread over several billets, return meant the family being split up, which could lead to upsets for the children. Frances Hardy describes what happened to her family:

My two brothers had been forced to return home rather suddenly. The lady of the house where they were billeted was unwell and it was decided that, as the air raids were less intense, in fact almost non-existent, they may as well return home. All this was explained in a letter that my mother wrote to Mrs Owen. Mrs Owen unfailingly read out to me exactly what mum said in her letters, this time it was, 'Ken and Arthur are coming home, but don't tell Frances because I want her to stay where she is for the moment.' Naturally I was far from pleased and quite convinced that nobody wanted me around. As usual that evening I helped with the washing up, and it wasn't long before I burst into tears, using the tea towel as a hankie!

For some, evacuation and return became almost a way of life; in Walthamstow, for instance, the record was held by one child who had left and returned no fewer than seven times. Such moves could be for a variety of reasons – Betty Goodyear explains how: 'Unfortunately, the lady of the family found that we were just a little too much work for her to cope with, on top of everything else, and we were transferred to a childless couple in a semi-detached house, who were also very kind to us.' Phyllis Wilkins moved six times in all: 'We had our own bedroom, I was seven years old and the bed was so big I couldn't get on it. I remember I had to go and sleep on my stomach every afternoon – I still don't know why. They were lovely to us, we even had nurses, but my sister got bored and ran away, so we were moved.' Lavender Clarke recalls how: 'They [the evacuees] stayed with us a long time. They had to go when the doodlebugs started; the military commandeered our farmhouse (or most of it, we got one room upstairs and one downstairs) and set up a searchlight.'

On 3 March 1943 there was an appalling accident at the Underground air-raid shelter in Bethnal Green. A sudden rush to enter the shelter caused a crush, and 173 people died, including 62 children under sixteen. The report on the accident concluded that one of the (several) causes was: 'The desire of parents to get their children under cover quickly, which induced numbers of people not hitherto users of the shelter to go there before a threatened raid. A very large number of children have fairly lately returned to the area. . . . The physical presence of large numbers of children who have come back recently to the area retarded the speed of intake into the shelter, and the speed at which people could reach it.'

FIVE

The Second 'Great Trek'

May–December 1940

In April 1940 the phoney war came to an abrupt end as Germany launched the Blitzkrieg. Denmark and Norway were invaded and Luftwaffe attacks on British coastal towns accelerated; it was in this month that the first civilian deaths in England caused by enemy aircraft occurred at Clacton-on-sea. On 10 May Germany invaded Belgium, Holland, France and Luxembourg; the last fell the same day, and within a week both Holland and Belgium had surrendered, but not before the centre of Rotterdam had been destroyed by the Luftwaffe. By 21 May German troops had reached the English Channel, and on the 27th the evacuation of the British Expeditionary Force from Dunkirk began. By 3 June it was all over, and on the 21st the French sued for peace.

The immediate invasion of Britain was widely expected, creating an impetus for fresh evacuations; some of the early reception areas on the east and south-east coasts were now likely invasion areas. On 19 May, 8,000 London and Medway children who had been evacuated to Kent, Essex and Suffolk were moved in sixteen special trains. Many LCC special parties had been moved to buildings in coastal areas, and it was decided that it was undesirable to continue to use premises between the Wash and Newhaven. Between 25 and 28 May nine such establishments, containing 1,500 children, were moved, along with their equipment, and were integrated into other existing establishments where there were vacancies. These were followed on 2 June by 48,000 children from nineteen east and south-east coast towns.

There was also, of course, a second reason for evacuation – bombing. Having conquered all its other enemies the Luftwaffe was now able to turn its entire attention on Britain, and flying from airfields in France and Norway meant that the whole of the country came within the range of German bombers, and even their short-range fighters could now operate over the south-east. The *Daily Express* of 31 May announced:

BOMB FEAR STARTS EVACUATION AGAIN

It was announced last night that the Government had decided to ask all parents in all evacuation areas – in Scotland as well as England – who wish their children to be evacuated to register them before the schools close on Monday afternoon.

Mr Malcolm MacDonald, Health Minister, in a speech last night, said the Government felt the risk of early bombing so real that they must now make as complete as possible the plans for evacuation.

New plans were hastily drawn up for the removal of school-age children, unaccompanied by their mothers, first from London and Thames-side, and then from the coastal areas of Norfolk, Suffolk, Essex, Kent, Sussex and Hampshire. Between 13 and 18 June 103,000 children were moved, including 61,000 from London where the schools were closed for a week, to Berkshire, Somerset, Devon, Cornwall and, in an extension to the LCC reception area, Wales. The lessons of the first evacuation were not ignored; every child was medically inspected the day before departure, by school doctors reinforced by GPs, dirty children were first sent to a hostel to be cleaned up before being billeted in private houses, and no child was allowed to join a party without a minimum outfit of clothing, any shortages being made up from clothes issued from a reserve depot. Mavis Kerr was one of those who took part:

I was evacuated from Dartford on 14 June with my school, West Hill. I was told by my parents the day before that I was going to be evacuated. My mother told me that I was to be a good girl and that I wasn't to cry.

A group of London infant schoolchildren evacuated to Sussex knit blankets for the troops, March 1940.

Evacuees and helpers leave Seaford, Sussex, in July 1940. With the fall of France, the south and east coasts became potential invasion areas and so were quickly evacuated.

Please keep this label in a safe place.
You will be told when it should be used
AND THEN IT MUST BE TIED
ON IN A VISIBLE POSITION
AND WORN BY THE PERSON
NAMED.

You will assemble
for Evacuation at

Christ Church School
ALFRED STREET

GROUP K

An evacuation label issued to Roy Judge when he was evacuated from Hastings in mid-1940.

We all queued up, we had our teeth looked at and our hair examined – prodded about for nits. Then we walked up the hill in the usual crocodile to Dartford station, where we caught a train to Waterloo.

This move was immediately followed by Plan V, known as the 'trickle' evacuation, made up of those children who registered late. Beginning on 7 July, by the beginning of August, 213,000 children, 112,000 from London, had been evacuated to safer areas. This only represented a small proportion of those eligible for the scheme; many children from the coastal areas took part but, once again, from the inland cities the take-up was, on the whole, poor.

The second stage of the evacuation was the removal of children who lived in the newly designated coastal evacuation areas – a total of thirty-one towns – to South Wales and the Midlands. To encourage this all the state schools in these areas were closed. John Kirk was among those who went from Clacton-on-Sea: 'I was evacuated to Burton upon Trent in the summer of 1940. When we got there we were taken to the Town Hall and then the Mayor, or someone like that, got up and said to us all, "You're here, we don't want you, but we've got to put up with you". Then we went to this hall and we were allocated;

"You're going to such and such road", and so on. I only stayed about three days.'
    In *Dover Front*, Reginald Foster describes the scene in that town:

> One of these rather sad days was Sunday 2 June. Many men from Dunkirk were
> still arriving, but the peak had been passed and it was time for the children to
> leave.
>   I was at the station that Sunday morning when the columns of marching
> children began to arrive. There were no crowds to see them off, no weeping
> mothers to make the parting harder. Approach to the station was closed, but
> even on the approaches there were very few parents and relatives . . . all the last
> kisses and final admonishments were got through at the points of assembly.

This was one of the lessons learned from the first evacuation; the crowds in the
stations had been compounded by numerous relatives saying goodbye to each
child, and the state of mind of the children on the trains had not been helped by
tearful partings as the train pulled out. It was decided to ask parents not to go to
the stations; those who did often found themselves refused access to the platforms
by the ticket collectors. Vera Biddle from Birmingham remembers this: 'I had
never been on a train before and our parents were not allowed to come to the
station. I remember feeling very lonely even though there were crowds of people.'
    Doreen Last recalls her experiences:

> In September 1940, when we returned to school after the summer holidays, we
> were summoned into the hall and told that the school – the Colchester County
> High School for Girls – was being evacuated. We had to meet at 9 a.m. the
> following day on Colchester North railway station. If we had younger brothers
> or sisters below school age our mums had to accompany us. My sister, aged five,
> was about to start school so mother came with us.

The situation in Colchester reflected what was happening in many of the new
invasion-threatened evacuation areas. In September 1940 a voluntary evacuation
scheme was introduced, of which 13,000 people took advantage, although by
Christmas most of these had returned. By March 1941 a new invasion scare was
at its height, and a second evacuation was planned; on this occasion only 200
people responded. In June the government issued an order under the Defence
Regulations for the compulsory registration of all children between the ages of
five and fourteen. These registrations continued until September 1943 when the
order was cancelled.
    Unlike the first evacuation, where most of the evacuees were transferred to
billets near their home town, many of those involved in this second transfer were
being moved far to the west, entailing a long train journey. The LCC and the
Ministry of Health asked the railway companies to provide hot meals and drinks
on such trips; the railway companies agreed, but on condition that the evacuation
helpers travelling on the trains helped serve the meals and wash up. This
finalised, the first hot meals, costing 1s., were served on 6 November; it was
further agreed that milk would be provided on shorter journeys.

Rochester children evacuated to Wrens Warren School in Ashdown Forest, 28 May 1940. (Kent Messenger Newspaper Group)

One of the more bizarre aspects of this second wave of evacuations was the removal, in June 1940, of livestock from vulnerable areas. Food rationing had been introduced in January, and the animals were regarded as too valuable a resource to fall into enemy hands should an invasion take place.

Plans were laid for the complete evacuation of the main coastal towns of West Sussex, East Sussex, Kent, and the south-east coast up to Southend – including Bognor, Brighton, Worthing, Ramsgate, Margate, Folkestone, Canterbury, Dover and Eastbourne. Almost ¾ million people would be evacuated over five days, using 1,000 trains and over 500 London Transport buses, with women and children travelling on the first two days. The winter of 1940 temporarily halted invasion scares, but with the arrival of spring 1941 they started again. The scheme, of course, never needed to be put into practice as Hitler decided to invade Russia. The plans were eventually suspended in November 1942.

Merseyside and the Midlands came under attack in August and early September. Frances Hardy went to Wales with a group of schoolchildren from Birkenhead: 'In August or September 1940 I was off again for a second evacuation which was to take me even further into the heart of Wales. My last memory of my departure from home is of Aunty Win on the platform handing me a small jointed doll dressed completely in knitted clothes which she had made herself.'

On 7 September, 1940, 'Black Saturday', the air assault on London began with a massed raid on the docks. Immediate steps were put in hand to re-evacuate the city. Londoners enjoying the traditional late hop-picking holiday were offered the option of transferring to a safe area instead of returning home; an offer that 8,000 took up. After the experience of the first evacuation, the population of London was now far more cautious, and response to the second wave was much slower; during September 20,500 unaccompanied children left the capital in organised groups.

Margaret Woodrow was a teacher in Middlesex: 'The school was not evacuated until bombing became more frequent. In October 1940 our evacuation was being arranged; rumours had it that we were going to Cornwall so I visited my parents in South Wales for the weekend. A few days later we passed through my hometown and arrived in Swansea!'

As the London docklands were pounded night after night, there were growing demands from social workers and community leaders that the docklands be declared Defence Areas, and that everyone not carrying out necessary war work be compulsorarily evacuated. The Bishop of London made representations to this effect to Sir John Anderson, now Minister of Home Security. However, a heavy decrease in the number of raids in 1941 made any such move unnecessary. The total of number of evacuees for the twelve months up to September 1941 was less than 60,000.

Later evacuation schemes varied from the original in small ways; one of these was the inclusion in the list of priority classes of persons made homeless by the bombing. However, would-be evacuees, other than children or mothers with children, had to provide evidence that they had a billet ready to take them.

In March 1940 unaccompanied children under five had been made a priority class. Some were war orphans, some had mothers who were working in the war factories and fathers who were in the forces. Vacancies in the evacuated nurseries could not satisfy demand, so new establishments were set up by authorities such as the LCC, or by voluntary bodies, or with money sent from America. Within a year 190 nurseries were available, capable of accommo-dating 6,000 children initially, and, by the end of 1942, up to 13,000. On reaching five, the children were transferred to ordinary billets. Children could be compulsorily evacuated if they were certified as suffering or likely to suffer in mind or body as a result of enemy attacks. In practice, these criteria were almost entirely used for children under five.

IMPORTANT NOTICE

EVACUATION

The public throughout the country generally are being told to "stay put" in the event of invasion. For military reasons, however, it will in the event of attack be necessary to remove from this town all except those persons who have been specially instructed to stay. An order for the com-pulsory evacuation of this town will be given when in the judgment of the Government it is necessary, and plans have been arranged to give effect to such an order when it is made.

You will wish to know how you can help NOW in these plans.

THOSE WHO ARE ENGAGED IN WORK OF ANY DESCRIPTION IN THE TOWN SHOULD STAY FOR THE PRESENT.

OTHER PERSONS SHOULD, SO FAR AS THEY ARE ABLE TO DO SO, MAKE ARRANGEMENTS TO LEAVE THE TOWN—PARTICULARLY
    MOTHERS WITH YOUNG CHILDREN
    SCHOOL CHILDREN
    AGED AND INFIRM PERSONS
    PERSONS WITHOUT OCCUPATION OR IN RETIREMENT.

All such persons who can arrange for their accommodation with relatives or friends in some other part of the country should do so. Assistance for railway fares and accommodation will be given to those who require it.

Advice and, where possible, assistance will be given to persons who desire to leave the town but are unable to make their own arrangements.

Information about these matters can be obtained from the local Council Offices.

(Signed) WILL SPENS.
Regional Commissioner for Civil Defence.

CAMBRIDGE.
2nd July, 1940.

(393/4177) Wt. 19544 30 125m 7/40 H & S Ltd. Gp. 393

An Essex coastal evacuation notice, July 1940.

Emergency Evacuation Schemes

On the night of 14 November 1940, Coventry was devastated by an air raid that lasted 11 hours and which destroyed over one third of the city's houses. The system that had operated up to this time for those made homeless – a short stay in a rest centre while the local council's billeting officer sorted out alternative lodgings – was completely inadequate when faced with a problem of this scale. The situation highlighted the need for the preparation of emergency evacuation schemes that could be initiated at very short notice, in response to similar heavy raids. In the days following the Coventry raid, other cities hastily cobbled together their own schemes; once in place, they were revised and perfected over the next few months. In *Hull at War*, Clive Hardy describes that city's emergency scheme: 'The headquarters from which the evacuation would be controlled were to be at Blenkin Street School, Witham, but if this building was damaged or destroyed, then Endike Lane School would be used. In the event of both of these buildings being unusable the headquarters would be housed at Bricknell Avenue School.'

This gives two insights into these schemes: first, the scale of damage involved – multiple alternatives were required – and, secondly, the important part that school buildings played. One advantage was that they were large buildings, and another, of course, was that evacuation was usually controlled by the local education officer, who would have been familiar with schools and their locations.

The Hull scheme continues:

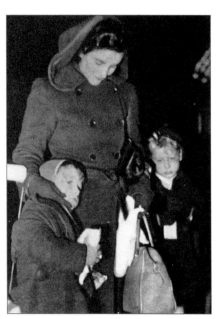

Parting – a young mother and her children, complete with labels, gas masks and bags. (HMSO)

The city was divided into ten divisions, each with a divisional headquarters and each divisional headquarters having three reserve headquarters. For example, Division One's headquarters were at Wheeler Street School. However, if this building was unfit for use, the first reserve was Paisley Street School. If Paisley Street was unfit then Francis Askew Boys and Girls was to be used, and if this too was damaged or destroyed, then the headquarters would move to Pickering Road School.

In turn, each division had a number of Reception Centres to which people in distress could be directed after an air raid. These centres, selected by the Air-Raid Welfare Committee, were equipped to process evacuees and arrange transport to the receiving depots from which people could then be found accommodation.

One last form of emergency evacuation was 'trekking', whereby, in an echo of the Paris scheme, citizens from heavily blitzed towns would tramp out of the area each evening to avoid the raids, often camping out in the surrounding countryside.

Overseas Evacuation

In the lead-up to the war some children were sent overseas privately, although the expense involved meant that this was an option only available to the wealthy, a cause of complaint among left-wing commentators. In 1940, following Dunkirk, many offers were made by Commonwealth countries and the United States to take evacuee children, and the government set up an overseas evacuation scheme, offering free passages for children (to be known as seavacuees) to the USA, Newfoundland and Canada. Sensitive to the earlier criticisms, a quota system was to operate; three-quarters of the children were to come from state schools. Some 200,000 applications were received by early July, and by 15 August the Children's Overseas Reception Board, CORB, based at Devonshire House, London, had approved applications for 19,365 children, 99 per cent of whom were attending state-aided schools.

It was a hard decision to make, to send your children to another country. Joyce Stockton from London *almost* became a seavacuee: 'Mother decided to have us two kids sent to Canada. We were scared as the train pulled into the station – never to see my three older brothers. Mother dashed onto the platform and dragged us away – we cried with joy.'

In August 1940 the first of a series of going-away parties was held for the departing seavacuees and their families at Grosvenor House in London. From this grew the 'Kinsmen', an association of parents who met to exchange letters, photographs and news of their children, and to provide entertainment and hospitality to American and Canadian service personnel.

One big drawback to overseas evacuation became obvious when, on 30 August 1940, the SS *Volendam*, carrying evacuees, was torpedoed and holed; a second torpedo failed to explode. The captain succeeded in transferring all his passengers by lifeboat to other ships, but two weeks later overseas evacuation ended abruptly with the sinking, on 17 September, of the SS *City of Benares* with the loss of seventy-three evacuees.

Betty Goodyear of Birmingham was one of those waiting to go to Canada:

Later, my sister and I were intended to go to Canada. We had been sponsored by a headmistress in Canada who was a friend of my headmistress at City Road Senior Girls' School and our passage was booked on the next ship to go. We had our inoculations and were waiting to hear our sailing date when news came through that a ship had been torpedoed and sunk with a load of children on board. Our ship, and the whole scheme, was then cancelled.

Betty Jones, in Tilbury, was also waiting: 'Mum and Dad filled in all the forms, and we went to a clinic for a full medical. We were told to pack our cases and that we would receive one day's notice. The cases were ready in the hall and then we heard the news about the *City of Benares*.'

There was no further official overseas evacuation, but the 2,700 children already sent remained abroad. In October 1940, the then Princess Elizabeth broadcast on the BBC's Children's Hour to children evacuated overseas: 'My sister, Margaret Rose, and I feel so much for you, as we know from experience what it means to be away from those we love most of all. My sister is by my side, and we are both going to say goodnight – come on Margaret! Goodnight, and good luck to you all.' At the beginning of the war, the princesses had remained in Scotland when the King and Queen returned to London.

The advent of clothes rationing caused a few problems for those going overseas. *The 1942 Clothing Quiz*, a pamphlet on clothes rationing issued by the Board of Trade, contained the following advice:

> Clothing supplies are needed for home consumption and there is now very little to spare. Shipping space is also severely limited. Accordingly, clothing should not be sent abroad unless it is urgently needed and supplies are not available locally . . . The Children's Overseas Reception Board will, on request, issue to parents a ration of sixty coupons per child to enable children evacuated to Canada, USA and Newfoundland and certain other countries to receive clothing from parents or guardians in this country.

Evacuation of the Channel Islands

Evacuation of the Channel Islands had already been considered as part of the general discussions of the subject pre-war, but no definite plans had been made.

An evacuation postcard – there were many such puns on the word.

On 16 June 1940, with France falling, the Home Office decided that there was no possibility of the islands being successfully defended, and it was agreed that they should be abandoned; the island authorities were informed of the decision on the 18th. The following day the local press announced the news and further reported that 'All children [are] to be sent to the mainland tomorrow – mothers may accompany those under school age.' Also to be included were men between twenty and thirty-three who wanted to join the forces, and others 'if possible'. Anyone wishing to go had to register immediately. The scale of the response varied; in Guernsey half the population went, whereas in Jersey the figure was only 20 per cent.

Eddie Roland from Guernsey clearly remembers this time:

June 19 1940 was a glorious summer's day, warm, hazy sunshine, blue skies, and not a cloud to be seen. Mum, my sister Joyce, and myself had spent most of the day on the beach at Fermin Bay. We were walking home along the fort road, chattering and laughing, when suddenly we saw, walking towards us, a lady who was obviously in great distress, crying, tears running down her face. We stopped, horrified, and Mum asked her what was upsetting her so much. Her answer was a body blow; 'Haven't you heard? We all have to leave the Island tomorrow. France has been taken.' She moved away, leaving us stunned with shock.

We hurried home to Dad and my sisters, Ruth and Marge. By the time we reached home, Dad already had the information given out by the authorities; all children had to report to their respective schools at 4 a.m. the following morning. Mum gathered together a few things for us, in brown paper carrier bags and we lay, fully clothed on our beds, waiting to report to our school in the early hours. We didn't sleep, we were still so shocked we hardly spoke to each other, just lay and waited.

The evacuation of children from Jersey began at 6 a.m. on 20 June. Enid Taylor lived in St Peter Port: 'We had to be at the school very early in the morning, I think about six o'clock, but for some reason we didn't leave that morning. We were sent home, to go back again the next day. We all went down to the harbour in Blue Bird buses. I remember singing "There'll be bluebirds over the white cliffs of Dover", not knowing what it all meant.'

Rozel Garnier was also evacuated from Jersey:

Above St Helier harbour there is an old fort, the battery. My father was caretaker and we lived there. When the Germans took France, the British army came and took over the fort, but they were only there for a couple of days. They told my father, 'We're leaving and you'd better come too.' I don't remember the journey over; I was up most of the night before queuing with my mother for tickets – you needed tickets for the evacuation.

Others evacuated from Jersey included the boys of the Army Technical School based in St Peter's Barracks. On 16 June they were moved to the Chateau Plaisir, a holiday camp, until arrangements were completed for their evacuation to the mainland, which they eventually did on the 19th, sailing for Southampton. The emergency nature of the move meant that little could be taken, as Pamela Buckley from Jersey recalls: 'We packed in great haste and took very little with us. At that tender age it was the toys we had to leave that hurt the most. I took just one doll. We went down to the pier and with hundreds of others in the same situation caught a very packed cargo boat.'

On Alderney, a hand-written notice from the Judge of Alderney, J.D. French, was posted on 22 June: 'I have appealed to [the] Admiralty for a ship to evacuate us. If the ship does not come, it means we are considered safe. If the ship comes time will be limited. You are advised to pack one suitcase for each person so as to be ready. If you have invalids in your house make arrangements in consultation with your doctor. All possible notice will be given.' The notice was given by church bells at 4.35 a.m. next morning, and the last ship left at noon.

There was concern that those of English descent would receive bad treatment from the Germans. Mrs R. Channing lived in St Helier, but was born in England: 'My husband went to England having joined the services in 1939. In his last letter he said to me: "Get out of the Island, you are English born." I was expecting twins any day. I managed to get away on an old boat, taking my two-and-a-half year old son.' Enid Taylor remembers: 'My father was English. Had he stayed in Guernsey, we feared he would be sent to a concentration camp.' There were other worries about staying on the islands too. Betty Collas was evacuated from St Helier in Jersey: 'I had an aunt who was seventeen, and there were stories going around about how the Germans treated women.'

A total of some 29,000 islanders took advantage of the offer of voluntary evacuation between 19 and 28 June before the islands eventually fell on 1 July. The whole atmosphere was one of rush and confusion. Roy Simon describes how his family were separated in the chase:

The time came to say good-bye to my parents and two younger brothers, then leave for the boat. All the children were crying, so were most of the parents. The boat trip is a bit of a blur. I can only remember noise, crying and confusion, with the teachers trying to pacify and control a large group of young children. Mum, Dad and my youngest brother Stan had been evacuated after us and sent to Huddersfield. My other brother Len was to travel with my maternal Grandparents, but the exodus became a shambles and they missed the last boat and had to stay in Guernsey for the rest of the war.

Eddie Roland endured an equally traumatic journey:

As the bus passed our little terraced house, I saw Dad watching for us, he waved – I didn't realise it would be five years before I saw him again. All the children had to be on the dock before 11 a.m. when we were able to board the ship – the *Felixstowe*, an ex-cattle boat – it looked pretty chaotic. While waiting, we saw the last of the resident troop of soldiers, which was the Irish Regiment, line up and board a ship, which set sail and disappeared in the distance. The ship finally started up and we slowly progressed out into the Channel. No one seemed to know where we were going and rumours were rife – some said America, others said Canada. Most of us had never left the island before. About halfway across the Channel we stared silently at the frightening sight of two sunken ships with their hulls sticking out of the water.

The boat trip from Jersey was not without incident either, as S.A. Yates recalls:

Somewhere towards mid-Channel my mother grabbed my arm and said, 'We've got to get below. Quick! There are German planes up there!' I looked up and saw two twinkling dots of light. I was really quite peeved at being hustled down the stairway, especially as rushing up the same stairs were three or four of the boy soldiers with looks of absolute glee on their faces; this was going to be their first sight of the enemy.

The Stukas attacked a French destroyer steaming about 500 yards off our port side. The destroyer put up a fierce counter-barrage, guns blazing, the bombs missed and the Stukas sheared away. Later we picked up four French soldiers rowing to England in a small dinghy. Our crossing had taken twenty hours, normal crossing time was less than ten; we must have zig-zagged all over the Channel.

Fred Bond remembers how: 'After we left Guernsey, I noticed a very drunk sailor at the stern of the ship with a small gun, there for our protection in case of attack! We hoped he wouldn't have to use it because he didn't seem capable of pointing it in any direction!'

The ships took the island evacuees to Weymouth, from where they were dispersed to various parts of Britain, mainly Scotland, the West Country, Lancashire, Cheshire and the West Riding. Here they were joined by other islanders to make up an evacuee community numbering almost 36,000.

Men arriving on their own were subjected to tight security checks. Fred Bond recounts his experience:

We were a mixed nationality group of men disembarking – tired, unwashed, unshaven, and black with coal dust. We were ordered to get in line and then checked by the Military Police who shouted. 'All the Irish over there.' The men who were prepared to enlist at once were escorted away. The rest of us were health checked and then taken to the old Alexandra Theatre, seated, and handed tea and meat paste sandwiches by the ladies of a voluntary organisation. This kindness was very much appreciated. When I got up to go to the toilet, a soldier, complete with gun, escorted me, stayed with me, and escorted me back. We were then taken to a school hall to sleep for the night. We slept on the floor and here I used a bun round I had got in Guernsey as a pillow. We spent a restless night and the following morning I ate my pillow! One at a time we went before a three-man tribunal, questioned – nationality, etc., and were we going to be chargeable on the Weymouth rates? I replied, 'If I can get to Taunton, I shall be OK.' Then the military guard was replaced by a police guard.

A Girl Guide helps evacuees from the Channel Islands. Evacuees were allowed to take one toy; the little boy on the right is carrying his.

Many Channel Island evacuees were sent to Bury in Lancashire. In a letter written in 1944, the Mayor of Bury described the changing community:

> At least one hundred and fifty children and their mothers were housed in new cottages on our Corporation estate in Chesham. Another fifty children from a home in Guernsey, along with master and matron and a staff of nurses, were comfortably placed in a large mansion house known as 'Danesmoor'. . . . Another group of children were housed in the neighbouring village of Tottington, fifty of them at Hollymount Convent, and thirty others in billets in Tottington and Greenmount.

Unlike mainland evacuees, those from the islands were almost completely cut off from members of their families who stayed behind. Eddie Roland comments that: 'After about twelve months we received a Red Cross letter from Dad. He was allowed 25 words which were typed on cream coloured strips stuck on to a piece of a paper. The words weren't important, they were censored anyway, but it was proof that Dad was still alive and that was the main thing. We started receiving 25 words every 6 months.'

A Channel Islands Committee was set up in London, under the directorship of Mr M.E. Weatherall, to oversee the social welfare of the community, and local Channel Isles Societies sprang up. Shirley Barry remembers some of the activities: 'My father played football for the CI society. I used to go round entertaining other CI societies, a group was formed and most children did something in the concerts.' Roy Simon recollects keeping in touch with other islanders too: 'The local group of Channel Islanders used to meet once a month in the town hall, to exchange news or share Red Cross letters. Every Christmas there would be a party and presents.'

EVACUATION OF GIBRALTAR

As well as the evacuees from the Channel Islands, a further 12,000 came from Gibraltar between July 1940 and July 1941. In May 1940, 13,000 Gibraltarian civilians had been evacuated to North Africa, mainly French Morocco, and Spain. Soon afterwards France fell, and in order to stop the French Navy falling into German hands, the Royal Navy and RAF attacked the French fleet. As a result, the Gibraltarian evacuees were subjected to all kinds of bad treatment by the French and were sent back home. In July 1940 ships began to take even more evacuees out of Gibraltar. Charles Trico was among them:

> We boarded the SS *Brittany*, a merchant ship that had only five cabins for the officers including the captain. Over 800 people were put in the ship's holds, in terrible conditions, lacking washing and toilet facilities. When we were sailing near the coast of Ireland, German planes bombed the convoy. I could actually see the planes, which were not flying very high, and also bombs falling astern of our ship. Luckily, no ships were hit and the attack was soon over.

Many of these evacuees were billeted in hostels in central and west London. Few spoke much English, and most of the children were taught in their hostels by London teachers. Henry J. Ramagge; 'arrived in the UK in 1940, where we were billeted in the Doctor Barnardo's home in Barkingside', and Charles Trico and his fellow evacuees 'were taken in trains to London, where parties of people were taken to different hotels which were prepared for our arrival. A number of us were lodged in the De Vere Hotel, and another, larger, party was in the Empire Hotel.' It was a cause of much dispute that the Gibraltarians were placed in the 'front line' of the blitz. Charles Trico continues: 'Soon after the night bombing started we youngsters were assigned to fire watch and several times we had to do so on the roofs of the hotel, trying to stop the incendiaries from taking hold, and many of these were picked up and thrown into the empty street below.' Henry J. Ramagge remembers similar concerns: 'Our school had no roof – it had been bombed – we had all our classes on the ground floor. We stayed there until the Doodlebugs started, then the men started to kick up a rumpus; we were told to pack, then we were taken by cattle boat to Downpatrick in Northern Ireland in July 1944. There we were put in a camp they had built; it was a row of Nissen huts in a field.'

The Gibraltarian islanders eventually began to return home in the summer of 1944. Henry J. Ramagge explains how: 'We were sent back to Gib right at the end of the war in May 1945, on the SS *Highland Monarch*. I remember the U–boats coming up and surrendering to our convoy.'

Although not strictly in the remit of this book, some mention should be made of the fact that there was also evacuation *into* Great Britain, in the form of 35,000 refugees from the continent, many of whom spoke little or no English. To deal with this, the WVS set up a 'Pentecost Brigade' of members who spoke European languages; these worked at the reception centres and the railway stations organising the refugees and sorting out problems.

SIX

The Third 'Great Trek'

July–September 1944

In the first three months of 1944 occurred what was known as the 'Little Blitz', a period during which more bombs were dropped on Britain than in the whole of the previous year; 90 per cent of these devices fell on London. Plans for an evacuation of schoolchildren were prepared, but the residents of London were more inclined to stay put and there was virtually no demand for it.

Information that Germany was preparing to launch 'rocket bombs' had begun to reach the British Government in April 1943; first reports suggested a weapon capable of delivering a warhead of between 5 and 10 tons, which would destroy every house within a quarter of a mile radius. The Cabinet set up the 'Rocket Committee', later the 'Rocket Consequences Committee', to look into what actions could and should be taken, including evacuation. Operational instructions were issued on 18 April 1944 dealing with 'pilotless aircraft', the first of which fell near Bow on Tuesday 13 June; two days later several more fell, starting a period of intense V1 'doodlebug' assault.

Late in 1943, the War Cabinet had decided that plans should be prepared to evacuate priority classes from Bristol, Cardiff, Dover and Plymouth. A scheme, codenamed 'Rivulet', was devised for the voluntary evacuation of schoolchildren, mothers with small children, and expectant mothers from London, Gosport, Portsmouth and Southampton following the start of a missile assault, or a re-commencement of heavy raiding. Within two days of the first V1 falling, a great deal of private evacuation began, but at first there was a distinct absence of any sign of an official scheme, causing a great deal of criticism. (One important reason for this delay was that the railways were needed to transport the vast amounts of men and materials needed to build the Normandy bridgehead.)

Registration for the official evacuation of schoolchildren from the affected areas eventually started on 1 July 1944, and the evacuation of these children began on 3 July – not until three weeks after the commencement of the V1 assault – and on 8 July registration of mothers and children got underway. Christine Pring from Sutton was among them: 'It was during the period of the Doodlebug attacks that my parents decided that my sister and I should be sent away from what was a danger spot. My mother must have been contacted by the authorities and agreed that it was a wise course. I am sure that they took into consideration that I was quite a nervous child, prone to singing 'Onward Christian Soldiers' through the night air raids – what a trial for everyone.'

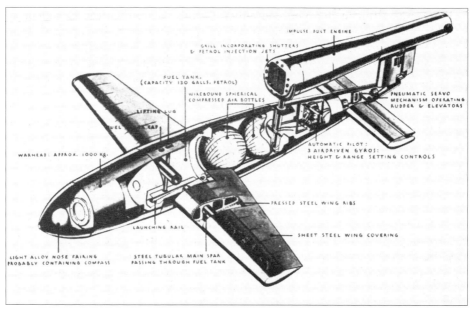

Diagram of a V1 from a magazine of the period.

Plans were pushed ahead, the evacuation areas were extended to include twenty-seven boroughs and urban districts around the Metropolitan area, and to the priority classes were added all mothers of school-age children. It was considered necessary to arrange temporary accommodation for 700,000 people in rest and reception centres within 40 miles of London.

Unlike earlier evacuations, this one had to be hastily planned and was carried out 'under fire', although there were no casualties during the actual evacuation. A WVS Station Marshal was in place at each railway terminus and WVS welfare workers travelled with parties. The evacuation areas were changed once again. Up to this point, one of the demarcation lines had been the Mid-Kent railway line, but now areas such as West Wickham were in the firing line. Birmingham, one of the original evacuation areas, became a reception area and in July, thousands of children from London and the South of England were evacuated there.

Winston Churchill made a statement to the House of Commons on 2 August 1944, in which he announced that the Government strongly advised those for whom official provision had been made, and also those with no war duties who could make their own arrangements, to leave the capital. The evacuation of hospital patients in the capital began immediately, firstly for their own safety, and secondly to free beds for the expected mass casualties. Throughout August a total of almost 16,000 patients was moved. By the end of August, 275,000 official evacuees had left London, although this number was dwarfed by the estimated 1.2 million who arranged evacuations privately. Phyllis Wilkins from Fulham and her family were part of this group:

There was a lull in the bombing and we came home; then the Doodlebugs started coming over. I was so frightened, I just about used to live in the shelter. Once one came down near us – the plaster came off the walls – we were surrounded by broken glass. My uncle came round and said to my mum, 'You've got to go away, Rose, you can't stay here!' We went to Gloucester again, to a place called Coney Hill, we had two rooms there.

Anne Peppercorn from Claygate also remembers leaving: 'I was about six when I was evacuated in the summer of 1944. We were on holiday in Cornwall, visiting my cousin who had been evacuated there, and I said how peaceful it was, away from the Doodlebugs – my parents arranged for me to stay there.'

By the end of August 1944 the tension began to subside as Allied advances on the continent were pushing German launch sites back. Plans had been laid for the complete evacuation of London, but as the attacks peaked, the plan was called off and those evacuation schemes not already in operation were cancelled. On 7 September, Duncan Sandys, in charge of the government inquiry into V weapons, announced to the press that the battle of London was all but over – the

The evacuation of children from Marian Vian School, Elmer's End, 1944. The V1 and V2 assaults of 1944 started a fresh round of evacuation. As with previous evacuations, the children have bags and labels, but notice the complete absence of gas masks. (Bromley Local Studies Library)

Kent children being evacuated in August 1944 from the V-weapon assault. (Kent Messenger Newspaper Group)

first rocket, or V2 as they were known, fell on Chiswick the following day. It seems amazing now, but on that same day the official evacuation scheme came to an end, although this did not apply to expectant mothers and unaccompanied children under five.

Once again, the return started sooner, and on a greater scale, than expected and by January evacuees were returning at the rate of 10,000 a week.

SEVEN
Arrival and Billeting

In the preceding chapters we have read how the great evacuation schemes were organised and accomplished. But the process didn't simply stop there. The evacuation having been on the whole, successfully completed, the process now shifted to the second stage, finding the evacuees places to stay. The problem centred around the need to house several million evacuees at short notice, and whereas in the sending areas the main pre-war task had been to encourage the people to evacuate, in the receiving areas it had been to find sufficient billets. This work began soon after the Munich Crisis, as many local councils sent out letters to all householders 'in order that you may be aware, in advance, of this enquiry and why it is being done' (Stroud UDC letter, January 1938).

The government leaflet *National Service*, published early in 1939, contained the following statement:

> The Government's plans for removing children in an emergency from the dangers of air attack in crowded cities to districts of greater relative safety would make an unprecedented call on the services of women. These plans for saving child life make it necessary to find homes for children, and any householder in these districts who has spare accommodation could do no more useful service in the national interest than undertake their care and maintenance.

Some householders were happy to accept evacuees but generally people were, understandably, reluctant to accept total strangers into their homes. It was realised early on that the scheme could not work on a voluntary basis, and that most people would only take refugees if compelled to do so, and if an allowance was paid. Billeting was made the responsibility of the local housing authority in the receiving area, who appointed local billeting

A newspaper appeal for foster parents.
(Crown Copyright)

officers to carry out the task of finding billets and allotting evacuees to them. Mary Noyle remembers how: 'Late one evening there was a knock on our door. It was a lady with a clipboard asking if we could take in a mother and her little boy, even for one night until more permanent accommodation could be found. We went into the street and there was this group of mostly children, clutching small suitcases or parcels and their gasmasks with labels tied to their clothes.' Local billeting officers had the power to force people to take evacuees if they had available space. Caroline Williams remembers one billeting officer:

One of the evacuated teachers was a young man and his new wife accompanied him. She had been a teacher but in those days a woman teacher had to resign on marriage. She was now employed as a billeting officer and, what we would call today, a social care worker for the evacuee children. She would appear at the classroom door with a large bottle of evil-smelling liquid and summon various children. Outside in the cloakroom she would anoint their heads with the liquid, for this was the nit-destroyer of the time. I never discovered what it was made of, which is perhaps just as well.

Linda Toomey became a billeting officer:

I was a newly qualified teacher given a tiring but necessary job of surveying the Epping area so that if children were to be moved from the London area, we would have places for them and their teachers and helpers. I was given a card which gave me power to billet anyone made homeless by bombing or evacuation. Of course, the evacuees were often helpful because the new mum would have more rations to spread among her flock.

In the cities the billeting officer was usually a local authority officer, but in the receiving areas the job was often done by a local 'bigwig'. Thus there was a criticism that many billeting officers tended to favour householders from the middle and upper classes, so that larger houses received, in proportion, fewer evacuees. A 1941 booklet for the guidance of billeting officers stated that: '. . . billeting officers should see that all houses, large and small, take in their share of evacuated persons.' This fair share was calculated on the basis of one person per habitable room; now there are rooms and rooms, of course, and officers were further instructed that they might exceed this figure in the case of 'exceptionally large rooms'.

Joyce Withers from Guernsey was billeted in a grand house:

The first house I was taken to was owned by a gentleman of means. I met him initially, then never saw him again. I lived with his 'butler', his wife and daughter. They seemed a nice family though. I was bought some lovely new clothes, a lovely royal blue hat and coat to match, and dresses, I'd never owned such nice clothes! The gentleman of the house had a lot of visitors, especially at holiday times, and his butler would have been extremely busy – so they got rid of me for a time, I was shunted off to another family for the duration of the holiday. This was rather unsettling for me, or so my headmaster and the billeting officer thought; they decided to take me away from them. All the clothes that had been bought for me were taken away, that made me so sad – it was rather a mean approach to a little girl, or so I thought – but they had bought them, after all.

Margaret Woodrow, a teacher from Middlesex, remembers how difficult it could be: 'Landladies found excuses not to take another evacuee when their evacuees moved back. Those free of evacuees were envied. I had four different billets in two years.' Margaret Durham also recollects people's differing attitudes towards taking evacuees: 'Some people were interested only in the cash, some refused to take evacuees, pleading age or infirmity or responsibility for relatives, but on the whole the situation was tolerated with good grace.' Householders could be exempted from taking evacuees on production of a medical certificate, although billeting officers could, at their discretion, choose to ignore this and order the householder to accept the evacuee, leaving the householder to appeal to a local billeting tribunal, who would hear appeals from both dissatisfied billeters and billetees alike.

Seaside resorts were widely used for evacuees because of the large amount of spare accommodation, with some groups being placed in holiday camps. Kathleen Corton's school went to one: 'We were taken to a holiday camp called the Corton Holiday Camp, the same name as mine; you know what kids are, I told the others that one of my relatives owned it.' It was soon discovered, however, that these

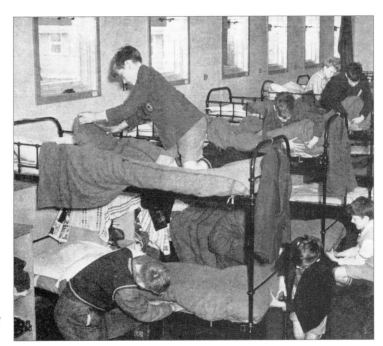

Boys from Beal Secondary School in camp school.

Camp school. (HMSO)

camps had been designed for summer use only, and a great deal of work had to be done to make them fit for year-round use.

There were also the camp boarding schools; before the war about twenty camps were run by local education authorities, either to provide working country holidays, or to be used as rest camps for weak or under-nourished children. The 1939 Camps Act allowed for the setting-up of up to fifty camps, each of which was to act as a holiday camp for 350 children in peacetime. In fact, thirty-one permanent camp boarding schools, or country camp schools, were constructed and financed by the government. These camps began to be completed early in 1940, and started to be used by local authorities as permanent boarding schools for children of secondary age. Progress was slow; by November 1940 only six camps were completed but by mid-1941, thirty of the camps were in use, housing over 6,000 children. The camps, set in country surroundings, had cedar wood buildings, including classrooms, dormitories, a dining room, hospital and a lavatory block. As well as the usual subjects, pupils were taught gardening, pig and poultry keeping, shoe repair and house management. The schemes were run by the local education authority of the city nearest each camp. Entire schools, children, teachers, equipment, were sent to the camps; some were for boys, some for girls, and a few were co-educational. Each housed about 250 pupils at a cost of around 25s a week each, although the parents were only charged the normal billeting fee for evacuees.

In many areas hostels were set up for senior pupils, which provided private study facilities. Where possible empty houses were requisitioned for use as billets – by 1943, 47,000 such residences had been requisitioned. Jean Garnham from Suffolk recalls such a situation: 'The local "big house" was Bawdsby Lodge. There was no-one living there so they billeted lots of evacuees there.' However, this scheme had its drawbacks, as Eddie Roland discovered: 'When we moved in, the house was completely empty, no furniture or floor coverings, so for a while we

Iris Miller (left) and her friend Doreen (centre) in the garden of their billet in Holcombe, Devon, with Iris's Aunt Kit.

Two badges given to evacuation workers: an evacuation nursery worker (left) and a Scottish evacuation hostel worker (right). There was a similar non-Scottish hostel badge; this was very like the nursery badge, but with the words 'evacuation hostel' on the cross-bar.

had to sit and sleep on the floor until friendly neighbours and the Salvation Army gave us some furniture and clothes. My bed was an old wooden frame with canvas lathes that sagged alarmingly in the middle.' There were more unusual billets too, as Ursula Nott describes: 'I took one family; as my house was already full I housed them in my caravan in the garden, where they were very happy.'

Later, several evacuation hostels were set up for younger children. Margaret Sudbury was a nurse in one at Pixton Park, Dulverton: 'It was like a boarding school for about seventy small children up to the age of five. I had a very big room with a double bed for myself, surrounded by eight little camp beds. We used to take them into the grounds, there were acres and acres of grounds. I remember being sent up from there to London to fetch two children down.'

However, in spite of all these measures, most evacuees were placed in private houses. Where unaccompanied children were billeted in private homes, the householders there were officially termed their 'foster-parents'. Blind adults were billeted in private homes, wherever possible in large towns where welfare support existed.

It was soon recognised that there some evacuees who were more 'difficult' than others; the Ministry of Health suggested that, in the first instance, a change of billet could be the answer. Bryan Farmer remembers 'Bailey': ' Bailey lived quite close to us, being billeted with a couple of Salvationists whom Bailey led a merry dance, even putting a hole in their tambourine and urinating into their tuba, an act so unforgivable that when reported to the billeting officer, he was moved to another part of town and I never set eyes on him again.' Should a move of billet fail, accommodation might be found in one of the 660 hostels operating by 1941. Then there were 'problem' children. These included children displaying behavioural difficulties, bed-wetters, and those termed 'skin cases', with skin complaints such as eczema. These children were generally placed in hostels run by teachers or specially appointed staff. The Ministry pointed out that: 'It is important that many different types of children presenting special problems should not all be collected in the same hostel.' Walter Hurst spent some time in a hostel: 'I was shunted about from family to family and landed up in a hostel, with thirty-nine other girls and boys, where I stayed for the rest of the evacuation. '

It was also difficult to house the physically handicapped. In these cases, hostels and camps again came into use; Margaret Sudbury worked as a nurse in one: 'When evacuation started I was at the Woodlarks in Surrey, a camp where crippled children would stay for a couple of weeks holiday to give their parents a break. Just before war broke out it was used to billet crippled young people from about seventeen up to their early twenties, from London and Birmingham. They slept in camouflaged army tents.'

Billeting Allowances

From the outset, 'billeting allowances' were paid to those taking evacuees and it was not unknown for unscrupulous householders to see evacuees as a source of money, and to cram in as many as possible. Another lucrative practice was to continue to claim for evacuees who had gone home. Billeting officers were advised to make regular visits to their evacuees to check on their welfare, but also to check that all evacuees being claimed for were, in fact, still in their billets. Should an evacuee choose to return home, the householder was supposed to hand the billeting notice back to the billeting officer.

The whole operation created a massive financial problem for the Government. The upkeep of the evacuees was costing £450,000 a week, and the maintenance of unaccompanied children about £250,000 a week – about £50,000 of this paid by parental contributions. Early in October 1939 it had been announced that, in future, parents must contribute towards the costs – 6s. a week out of the estimated cost of 9s. – and from 28 October, those who could afford it were to pay the full amount. It was accepted that not all parents could afford to pay; parents were means tested, which resulted in a quarter of all parents paying nothing.

At first billeting allowances were paid to householders at the rate of 10s. 6d. a week for the first child, and 8s. 6s. each if more than one child was billeted. In

An LCC 'Repayment of Billeting Charges' form dated November 1939 informing Mr Ryall that he will be charged 6s. for each of his two children.

October a flat rate was introduced of 10s. 6d. for all unaccompanied children who had reached the age of sixteen, lowered in February 1940 to fourteen. By 1941, the following comprehensive billeting allowances were being paid: for mothers accompanied by children, for 'invalids', 'cripples', the blind, the aged and homeless persons – 5s. a week for an adult and 3s. a week for each child under fourteen, and 5s. each for any over fourteen. For unaccompanied children there was a sliding rate depending on their age: for those under ten – 8s. 6d. a week was paid (where there was only one child it was 10s. 6d.); children between ten and fourteen, 10s. 6d. a week in all cases; between fourteen and sixteen, 12s. 6d. a week and sixteen and over, 15s. a week. Local authorities were also empowered to compensate householders whose furniture or bedding was damaged by evacuees.

Official helpers were entitled to be billeted at a rate of 21s., as long as they worked full-time as helpers. They were also entitled to receive a certain number of vouchers for cheap or free travel for the purpose of visiting their evacuation area. Teachers evacuated with an organised party were entitled to free billeting, or money in lieu of billeting allowance, if they made their own accommodation arrangements.

Expectant mothers who took part in the official scheme were normally evacuated in the last month of pregnancy, and were billeted close to a maternity hospital, to be transferred there as soon as necessary. If, however, the confinement took place in the mother's billet, an extra 10s. a week was payable to the householder for the two weeks following the birth, although this could be extended, if necessary. Some expectant mothers were evacuated earlier. These women were mixed in with the mothers with children until it was time to go to the maternity hospital.

All this was, of course, pre-National Health Service, and all medical treatment had to be paid for, but arrangements were made with the medical profession to treat evacuated children without charge to the foster-parents, although local authorities were encouraged to set up sick bays 'for minor cases of illness which cannot conveniently be treated in billets'. They were also authorised to pay foster-parents an allowance of 5s. a week for nursing an unaccompanied child through a minor illness. More serious cases would be treated, free, in the local hospital. Other arrangements were sometimes made – Miriam McLeod recollects that: 'I got measles. I had to leave the billet and stay with the billeting officer.'

Clothes and shoes remained the responsibility of the parents, although separation, and in many cases lack of funds, made this difficult. Jennifer Satchell remembers her grandparents' evacuees at their farm in Egleton, Rutland:

> They arrived carrying a small suitcase. In fact, they had practically nothing, other than what they stood up in. One garment they did have, were combinations. These were woolly undergarments comprising a top with sleeves, joined onto leggings, with a slit in the bottom area, which really amused my sister and me. For the life of me, I cannot remember how they got into them. The next day my grandmother took them into Oakham to get them clothes suitable for life on a farm.

The Ministry of Health recommended that: 'The first step towards keeping the unaccompanied children properly clothed and shod is for their own teachers to hold regular kit inspections. Once a week is not too often.' If repairs or replacements were found necessary, the parents would be contacted. Where the parents were 'unable or unwilling' to provide replacements or money (and, of course, ration coupons), the local authority in the sending area was to provide them. The sending authorities were also supposed to check that unaccompanied children were suitably clothed and shod on arrival in a reception area. Clothes might also be provided through the WVS County Clothing Depots, or through make and mend parties in the receiving area.

It was even more difficult for the children evacuated from the Channel Islands. Joyce Withers from Guernsey remembers: 'The Red Cross supplied us with clothing, so every six months or so we were given a list (by the people we lived with) of clothes we were short of, and after school we'd meet in a special classroom and our Guernsey teachers would outfit us as best they could.'

Arrival

Those evacuated by rail would arrive at railhead stations, and from there be dispersed, usually by bus, to the towns and villages. For instance, in south-east

Birmingham evacuees arriving in Gloucestershire. Notice the two 'treasures' standing in the window.

Essex, Colchester St Botolph's station was the railhead for 14,000 evacuees to be dispersed into the neighbouring districts, 5,500 to the Lexden and Winstree district, 5,500 to Tendring, 1,600 to Brightlingsea, 900 to West Mersea and 500 to Wivenhoe.

On arrival the evacuees were taken to central clearing points; in Redhill, Surrey, this was the Odeon Cinema; in Sevenoaks, Kent, it was the pens of the cattle market. Then they were fed and issued with emergency rations for 48 hours. In Stroud this consisted of 1 can of meat, 2 cans of milk, 1 lb of biscuits, ¼ lb of chocolate, all packed in a carrier bag – adults received an extra can of meat. Mavis Kerr clearly remembers her arrival at Launceston: 'There to greet us were two zinc baths, one was full of buns, which I later found out were saffron buns – I loved them – and one was full of lemonade.' Betty Goodyear from Birmingham had a similar experience: 'We boarded a train in Birmingham and travelled to Newport, where I remember we were taken to a biscuit factory and given a tea in the works canteen. I remember corned beef sandwiches (we seemed to almost live on corned beef for the whole of the war years) and loads of biscuits, which seemed marvellous to me, and pop.' But it wasn't all good food, as Eddie Roland explains: 'Once settled, nuns came in with bowls of "Irish stew", which had a horrible burnt taste. It was only years later that I discovered that Irish stew wasn't supposed to taste like that.' Other needs were also catered for. Audrey Arnold recalls how: 'When the train arrived at Alconbury station there were two lines of toilets set up for us, made of sacking and stuff, one for the girls and one for the boys.'

Clarice Ruaux from Jersey describes her experience:

After breakfast we were just sitting in this hall wondering what was going to happen, and some ladies came into the hall and a couple of them came up to Edie, Mum and I and said, 'Would you care to come home, and have a wash and that, or a bath if you like.' We said that would be marvellous – I've never been so filthy in my life. Coming along in the train, we'd stop in the stations and people would hand in bottles of water and the children would get hold of them and, of couse, it would get spilt, and there wasn't a corridor on the blooming train. So here we were, terribly grubby, and we went to their home, which was just like a palace, and we had a lovely bath, one after the other and then a lovely cup of tea or coffee – it was marvellous.

Arrival did not always go as planned. Often the journey took far longer than expected so that by the time the evacuees arrived it was too late for them to be billeted. This happened to S.A. Yates:

The train was hours late. In those days there were chocolate vending machines on the station platforms, you put two pence in the slot and got a bar of Fry's chocolate – the one on the platform was empty. I must have gone to that machine a hundred times during the next few hours in the hope that the man would come and fill it up. When the train did arrive it was packed solid! Civilians, army, navy and air-force all moving westwards. We squeezed into the corridor and there we stayed; once you found a square foot to stand you were there and you couldn't move. The journey took hours, we would travel for

Birmingham evacuees boarding buses at the railhead in Stroud.

twenty minutes and then stop for half an hour at signals, and so on time after time. The railway timetable must have been in chaos that day.

Sometimes temporary accommodation had to be arranged for the first night, as Betty Jones remembers: 'At Yarmouth we were taken to a primary school where we were sorted into classes and bedded down on sacks of straw – they smelt foul. I remember the headmistress coming round in her dressing gown.' Doreen Last also spent a night 'sleeping rough': 'We got off the train too late to be billeted out, so we were taken to a school, during an air raid. Everyone was given two blankets and we used our luggage for pillows and "slept" on the hall floor. The windows had no blinds so searchlights, flashes, and fires were visible all night.' Sometimes this could go on for some time, as Iris Gent found out: 'We went to Little Catfield; about ten of us were put in a sort of outbuilding. We slept on sacks on the floor and had our meals in a sort of garage. This went on for about four weeks.'

Ourselves in Wartime contains the following, official, description of the evacuees' arrival: '. . . the country was expecting them. Plans had long been made for their reception. Tea was waiting for the children in village halls. Local billeting officers had found billets in cottages, farms, and manor houses for the children; when they had had something to eat, the children recovered their high spirits, and were taken by car or lorry to their new billets.' In reality, it was rarely that simple; as I have said previously this phase of the operation was relatively new, and it is therefore understandable that it was less well organised than the transport side. Margery Allingham's book *The Oaken Heart* tells the war-time story of Tolleshunt D'Arcy, and the following description of the arrival of evacuees highlights how this part of the procedure was not always organised as well as it might have been:

A message came from the Lion to say that eight buses were on their way. This delighted us all, and Mrs Moore got the kettles boiling. We were fidgeting about making last minute preparations, when Doey, who had been thinking over the message, suddenly said 'Eight buses?'

I said, 'Oh, they'll be those little old-fashioned char-a-banc things.' And he said, 'Very likely.'

I was wrong. Mrs Moore, who was by the big window which looks on the road, saw them first. There they were as foreign-looking as elephants. There were eight of them, big red double-decker London buses, the kind that carries thirty-two passengers on each floor, and as far as we could see they were crowded. They pulled up, a long line all down the road, with a London taxi-cab behind them. A small army of drivers and officials sprang out, shouting instructions at their passengers.

It was at this point that Doey made the second discovery. They weren't children. They were strange, London-dressed ladies, all very tired and irritable, with babies in their arms.

The simple fact is that, for a long time, evacuation was seen purely as an exercise in emptying the cities – the very word evacuation, meaning to empty,

An al fresco classroom. (HMSO)

clearly demonstrates this. Thus the emphasis at the 'sending' end was to pass on the evacuees as quickly as possible. As soon as groups arrived at the various stations and railheads, they were put on the first available train, with no reference to where they were going, or to who was being expected at the other end. Joyce Fry experienced problems – 'Somehow we did not reach the station in time to catch the Huddersfield train on which we were supposed to be travelling, so another batch of children went there, while we ended up in Leeds' – as did Eddie Roland from Guernsey: 'After a 22-hour journey, we pulled into Glasgow – so much for our identification labels giving my aunt's address in Portsmouth!'

The Schools in Wartime, published in 1941, describes the problem this made for school parties:

> Working against time and the possibility of air attack at any moment, it was not possible to secure that the school parties all reached destinations where suitable, or in some cases even sufficient, school accommodation was available. This was the case more particularly with the London and Greater London groups, covering some half of the children evacuated, for whom the transport arrangements were necessarily very complicated. As a result, some Secondary and Junior Technical Schools found themselves decanted in remote areas out of reach of any local school of similar type; while other schools found themselves scattered over a wide area in a number of villages.

The problem was more marked for secondary schools, which had far larger rolls, and needed more specialised facilities than primaries. Most villages had their own primary school and the younger evacuees could be absorbed into them. A further factor was that a larger percentage of secondary age children were evacuated. Over the first few weeks, a great deal of work was done to relieve the situation; many parish halls, large houses and buildings of all sorts were pressed into temporary use, and a certain amount of re-billeting went on. The experiences of Croydon children, as described in *Croydon and the Second World War*, are typical: 'For weeks in some cases, teachers and children assembled at some agreed point and walked the country lanes until they could be housed in some suitable hall. And what a variety of buildings were used! A Salvation Army Citadel; a Church of England hall; a hall behind a public house; two St John's Ambulance halls and several derelict schools and village halls were taken.' By Christmas 1939 the problem was widely accommodated, if not solved. This may seem a long time, but it was not so bad as it seems. At first the majority of teaching was carried on outside, in the fields, or on the beaches, with a great deal of nature study, and for the urban evacuees during that fine autumn, this was new and interesting stuff. Schools treated the situation as if they were on a huge school trip, which in effect it was. It also has to be borne in mind that those who remained in the cities fared worse. Most schools were not re-opened before Christmas, and in some places not until April.

The organisation of school parties owed much to the accompanying teachers. *Ourselves in Wartime* describes some of their work:

When the school parties arrived at their country destinations and were taken to their billets, it was the school teachers who had to go round the town, seeing that each child was safe; and when they returned to their own billets – not always so comfortable or happy – there might be a frantic inexperienced 'foster mother' waiting with an hysterical child she could 'do nothing with'.

Hot meals at lunch time were organised for the children in the schools, and for fourpence the children could have a nourishing and appetising meal. But it was the school teacher who had to supervise it; gone was the pleasant lunch hour in the staff room. And the evenings were occupied with filling in a shower of forms which descended from every department . . . clinic forms, milk forms, canteen forms, clothing forms, national savings forms . . . to say nothing of writing to parents.

Roy Simon describes how some Guernsey teachers became foster parents: 'We were shared out among the teachers; I was allocated to Miss Parker along with some classmates. When we landed at Weymouth we boarded a train and started a long journey to Bury, Manchester. On arrival we were found accommodation and our group was billeted with Miss Parker in a house in Goldfinch Drive.' Iris Gent from Greenwich sums up the part played by the teachers: 'They were wonderful, those teachers, evacuation would never have worked without them.'

Then it was the task to sort out individual billets. This was accomplished in various ways, by far the most common of which is described in the following recollections. Frances Hardy from Birkenhead:

We arrived at our destination sometime in the afternoon. I suppose there must have been twenty or thirty children of different ages brought to the hall that day. Marjorie Woodward and I were two of them. Marjorie had been given strict instructions by her parents not to be parted from me, no matter what we were to be billeted together.

We were all made to walk around the hall and wait for somebody to lay claim on us – what a sorry sight! All that clomping around on a planked floor with cardboard-boxed gas masks over our shoulders! Several times during this parade somebody came over to whisk me away with them only to be confronted by my little friend, who had had her orders not to be parted from me. The inevitable happened; when all the other children had been claimed there were just two left – the ones who were not to be parted. We were eventually taken to a cottage in the village to live with the Owen family.

Phyllis Wilkins from Fulham: 'At the end of 1940 my sister and I were sent to Guildford, we went by coach with other evacuees. When we got there, people came up and said, "I'll have you", "I'll have you", and so on.'

Small, 'cute' children were often snapped up, while older siblings were harder to place. Christine Pring from Sutton remembers how: 'We were all congregated in the Town Hall, where people, our prospective carers, came to pick the most likely. Our little four year old was chosen immediately by the County Sanitary Inspector (who I thought must inspect lavatories). My sister and I came as a job lot so no doubt we were difficult to place. However, we eventually left with a plump, very Lancashire lady.'

Fitting in with the billeter's own children was another reason why some were chosen. Betty Jones has memories of: 'the usual slave market; a lady with a cocker spaniel and a little girl aged five took me. She was horrified when she found out I was nearly ten, she wanted me as a companion for her little girl!' Kathleen Corton recalls how: 'Mum said we weren't to be separated; when we got there the people came round and chose us – one lady wanted me to be a companion for her daughter who was about my age, but I said I couldn't go without my sister. She didn't want to take her, but in the end she said my sister could come but I would have to be responsible for her.'

Betty Gagg and her family, from Galmpton, Devon, took in evacuees, and saw the situation from the other side of the fence: 'When it was time to collect our sole evacuee my mum said one girl only, but on arriving at the village hall there were five hundred evacuees, among them Rose and Ivy, two sisters from Walworth – not to be parted. So home they came!' Sometimes there were genuine problems. Iris Gent experienced one: 'The billeting officer took me to one woman, but she said: "I can't take a big girl like you. I have to bath my husband in front of the fire!"'

Although, for propaganda reasons, it was reported at the time that 'no one was lost', this was not strictly the case, as Joyce Fry explains:

A lady came and took my brother and I; she did not sign for us, and we learned later that the billeting officer was frantically trying to find these two children who were still unaccounted for on his list. Our new 'Auntie' hadn't got any idea how to look after us – we had Rowntrees fruitgums for breakfast. A cat walked around on the table whenever there was food about. We were there for three days. My brother slept on the floor covered with coats, I had to sleep with 'Auntie'. It was extremely frightening when we witnessed the row on the arrival of the billeting officer when he finally tracked us down. Whenever this time was mentioned to adults there was a quick 'Ssshh'. Eventually my mother explained that our 'Auntie' was a prostitute. She was actually very kind to us, so she probably just wanted someone to love.

There were often a few evacuees left over at the end for whatever reason; large families could be difficult to place, as Miriam McLeod from Clapton discovered: 'no one would take three sisters, so my eldest sister, Ruth, and I went to one billet, and my middle sister, Shirley, went to another.' The effect on the children was often terrifying, as Walter Hurst from Birkenhead recalls: 'As time went by my sister and I were left with only one other boy and girl, sister and brother. We thought nobody wanted us and were very frightened. At last a lady came forward and said, "I'll take the two girls – I don't like boys." Then her sister said, "I'll take the two boys." Thus we were split up from our sisters, all very unsettling for nine year olds.'

In situations like these, the billeting officer came into her own. Vera Biddle from Birmingham recalls her experience: 'When we arrived at Maesteg we were all gathered into a school hall for biscuits and cocoa. Then local people came to collect a child. After a long time there were a few of us left. We were taken in a car (I'd never been in one of those) and the lady with us knocked on a few doors. I was getting worried as it was dark by then, but eventually I was taken in for the night – and I stayed there for nearly three years.' Joan Rands from Ipswich remembers 'a bus load of London refugees arriving, unannounced, at our little private primary school in Bucklesham Road. Without warning, my grandmother, who lived opposite the school, had twin girls named Daisy and Violet foisted upon her.'

Sometimes things were better organised and the billeting officer would allocate evacuees direct to billets. Roy Proctor from Felixstowe remembers how: 'The billeting officer came round and asked "How many can you take?" We lived in a big, draughty old house at that time with four bedrooms; my mother had two boys from East Ham, brothers by the name of Cribb.' Jane Black from Bacton also recalls the role played by the billeting officer: 'We had a billeting officer in the village who came round and assessed all the houses for how many evacuees they could take. My mother and father-in-law had four little girls from London, two sets of sisters, in the farmhouse, and I had a teacher in my house. They were all very nice, the teacher would often bring the other teachers over for a cup of tea.'

Not all evacuees were small children: Betty Rolfe, aged sixteen, from London, billeted in Stoke-in-Teignhead, on a visit to nearby Torquay.

Lavender Clarke recalls what happened in Eastbridge, Suffolk: 'I don't think mother

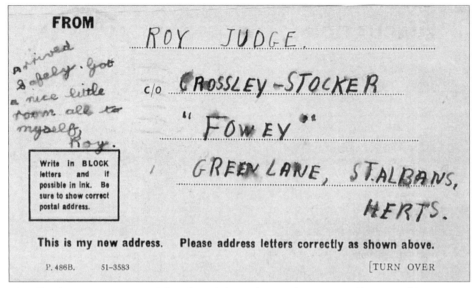

An official evacuation postcard from Roy Judge, informing his parents of his new address. Notice Roy's added note: 'Arrived safely. Got a nice little room all to myself.'

St John's CE School. A notice is pinned up to inform parents where their children have gone. Changes to schedules meant that parents did not know in advance where their children were going – neither did the children! (Crown Copyright)

" *Here's sixpence.   Go and evacuate*
yourself."

Woods' cartoon from The Black-out Book.

knew they were coming 'til the day before they arrived. They just came round in a van saying, "You've got to take four" and so on.' In Colchester, things were even more organised. Doreen Last describes the system used: 'Billeting officers called, giving out sets of large red numbers and black numbers to be displayed in our front windows as to the number of people living in the house and the number of bedrooms. We were compelled to have an evacuee – my sister had to move into my bedroom.' Mary Spink from Wells End remembers the evacuees who stayed with her mother: 'My mother took two little evacuees in her cottage. I was working in another house and my neighbour came and said, "You've got two little sisters", I said; "I didn't know she was pregnant!"'

Obviously, parents had not been told in advance where their children would be taken, so, on arrival at their new billets, the first job for the children was to fill in a postcard so that anxious parents would know where their children were, and that they were safe. Joyce Fry explained how: 'We had a piece of Victoria sponge and a glass of milk before finding out why we had a postcard in our case. Our new "Auntie" wrote her name and address on the back, and we walked to the post box to send them home, so that Mummy and Daddy would know where we were.' Back in the cities notices were posted outside the schools telling parents where their children had been sent.

EIGHT

Billet Life

The first evacuation was a press photographer's dream – the fine weather, the countryside at its most beautiful, and, of course, cherubic-faced children. Added to this was the delightful scenario of city children being introduced for the first time to the rustic delights of fields, cows, sheep, black-berrying, and so on. The images produced helped to reassure parents, many of whom were separated from their children for the first time.

There were many humorous references to the town child's view of the country. The 9 o'clock news of 29 October 1939 ended with the reading of an essay written by a ten-year-old London evacuee:

> The cow is a mammal. It has six sides, right, left, an upper and below. At the back it has a tail, on which hangs a brush. With this it sends the flies away so that they do not fall into the milk. The head is for the purpose of growing horns and so that the mouth can be somewhere. The horns are to butt with, and the mouth is to moo with. Under the cow hangs the milk. It is arranged for milking. When people milk, the milk comes and there is never an end to the supply. How the cow does it I have not yet realised but it makes more and more. The cow has a fine sense of smell, one can smell it far away. This is the reason for the fresh air in the country.
>
> The man cow is called an ox. It is not a mammal. The cow does not eat much, but what it eats it eats twice so that it gets enough. When it is hungry it moos and when it says nothing it is because all its inside is full up with grass.

Margaret Watling describes 'her' evacuee:

> Then along came Jimmy, aged nine, from 'Wandsworf', thin, pale, and scared. Having fed, scrubbed, and de-nitted him, Blanche and I did our best to put him at ease, and were rewarded with his appreciation and humour. Jim's pal was 'Breamy' and together they regaled us with tales of their exploits at home, street football and fights. Like other city children they knew little about the countryside and were surprised to discover the origins of milk, eggs, bacon, bread, etc.

And Lavender Clarke remember hers: 'They were nice kids, they grew to like the country, although it was very different from what they were used to, milk from a cow instead of a bottle, walking around in welly boots, a mile walk to school.'

Southwark Central schoolgirls working on the land, Newton Abbot. (Crown Copyright)

Betty Robinson recollects her impressions of the farm she was sent to: 'The farmer let us do little jobs on the farm, all very different from our house in Greenwich. We gave all the animals names, and saw a horse have her foal – our first lesson on how babies arrive.' Edward Harrington from Felstead, Essex, remembers how: 'We had two evacuees, Reggie Merril, aged eight, and his sister Joan, about nine. They thought it was just wonderful to be out in the country – they'd bring five or six of their friends over at the weekend. My father kept bees and they loved honey. There was a farm over the road, the farmer used to set rabbit snares, and Reggie learned to do this from the farmer.'

Yet behind these innocent memories and reflections lay many very real problems, which were the results of deep-seated cultural differences between the urban and the rural, which were far more pronounced at that time, before television, travel and the growth of urbanisation had ironed out regional differences. Accents could prove difficult; Mavis Kerr clearly remembers her arrival at Launceston: 'Aunt May had a broad Devon accent; at first I couldn't understand a word she was saying and she couldn't understand a word I was saying.' Eddie Roland had a similar problem in Glasgow: 'On arrival we were met by a group of people chattering away in a foreign accent. We honestly couldn't understand a word, but I think they were offering us accommodation.'

One particular problem sprang up in North Wales. Many children were evacuated there from England – they, of course, spoke English, where many of

The Evacuees.

If you have any young evacuees billeted on you, do teach them the difference in the hedge berries. The privet berry is *not* a blackberry, although it is dangerously like. It is a berry and it is black, yet it is not a blackberry! Also it is safe to warn them that no *red* berry is fit to eat at all! A friend of mine who spends her life doing good works has written me the sweetest, almost poetic, letter about the joy of getting children into safety and beautiful surroundings. I should like to say a few words from the other end. But perhaps it would not be politic or even kind!

ELVIRA.

An article from the Bromley edition of the Kentish Times, *dated 6 October 1939, highlighting some of the dangers facing city children in the countryside.*

'Vacuation' cards, a variation on the card game 'Happy Families'. These Householder cards show two stereotypical rural billeters.

YOUR EVACUEES!
Extra mouths to feed
To make the most and get the best
out of every scrap of meat
use

BISTO

A Bisto advert – feeding evacuees could be a constant problem.

their hosts spoke Welsh. Often the schools helped, visiting and home teachers swapping for a day, so that the evacuees were taught in Welsh, which added to the Welsh they were picking up as they went along, as children do. Walter Hurst from Birkenhead recalls how: 'My sister stayed with "her" family who spoke nothing but Welsh and she learnt to speak the language like a native.' Betty Goodyear also picked up some of the new language: 'Our teachers taught us to sing the Welsh national anthem in English so that we could know what the words meant.'

A cause of many early problems was, as every parent would guess, food, and here the regional differences really came into play. Betty Gagg remembers her evacuees: 'For their first meal my mother had made a roast, and there was that well-known Devon dish of Junket for afters   no way would they eat it, they wanted cow heel. My mother said "Eat it or go hungry." They stayed – and ate everything!' Christine Pring recalls her first meal: 'I remember we had dinner in what to us was a very strange order; gravy and Yorkshire pudding, then meat and vegetables, followed by fruit cake. My sister told the lady of the house that she only liked chips, quite untrue of course, so we proceeded to have them every day, and consequently blackheads as well!' On the whole, the evacuees, including Walter Hurst, soon began to enjoy the country food: 'I, who had been very difficult over food at home, learned to eat anything and everything. We had cake once a week on a Sunday. Plenty of milk and good home-grown vegetables, especially broccoli and beetroot! Very few sweets or sugar.' Betty Goodyear also has fond memories of the food: 'The cooking was wonderful and I can remember how amazed I was to see apple pies and egg custards that were 4 or 5 inches deep.

Farmhouse cooking of course!' Phyllis Wilkins remembers: 'a nice little country cafe with about six or seven tables. There was a lovely lady there; she used to make really big pasties, I used to go and get one for us all.' Sometimes it worked the other way, as Caroline Williams explains: 'We had evacuees from Birmingham, many of whose parents worked in the Bourneville chocolate factory there and when they visited their children they brought bags of misshapen chocolates which were very much appreciated.'

Religion also posed a potential problem, and little effort had been put into matching the evacuees with the billets in this respect. Iris McCartney remembers how: 'I was evacuated the weekend the war broke out with my school, St Edmund's RC Juniors; I was nine years old at the time. First of all they took us to Blockley, but there was no Catholic church there, so after a few weeks we were sent over to Stow-on-the-Wold.' Mavis Kerr commented that: 'They [her foster-parents] were Methodists, so we used to go to the Methodist Chapel, I was C of E, but Mum told me to do as I was told, so I went. I rather enjoyed the Methodist meetings; chapel in the morning, Sunday school in the afternoon, chapel in the evening.' Often ways were worked out to try to accommodate the newcomers, as happened to Walter Hurst: 'When we first went to Harlech we were amazed at the number of chapels: Calvinistic Methodist, Wesleyan Methodist, Baptist, Congregational, and – surprise – Scottish Baptist! We were invited as a group to each church on a rotation basis where they would hold an English service to accommodate us.' Betty Gagg's family also tried to help: 'We had another two sisters, Ruth and Dorothy Daley, from Bromley in Kent, who stayed a long time. They were Roman Catholics, and we were Chapel, so we all went on alternate Sundays to each other's church.'

Jewish evacuees from London's East End and other areas faced particular problems, as Miriam McLeod found: 'In Bishops Stortford they used to send us to the Synagogue on Saturday and then we went with them to the church on Sunday. We went because we'd been told to do as we were told; early in the war the Chief Rabbi had broadcast on the radio to say it was alright for evacuee Jewish children to eat pork.' June Cohen remembers:

Although we were Jewish my older brother told me to eat everything I was given; I had to survive. I remember I didn't though; once, we were taken for a walk in the woods, and a teacher told us that rabbits and hares were the same family as cats [!]. Later we were given rabbit stew – I couldn't eat it – I thought, cat! We didn't go to Synagogue at all, I went to church with the family I was billeted with. It was the first time I had gone to a church; they were all praying to God and I wondered who God was. I was in the Guides in Luton; one day they had a church parade. They said anyone from a different denomination didn't have to go, but I did, I didn't want to stand out.

The lack of modern amenities was often a shock for the evacuees. Iris Tilman remembers: 'It was a strange place after London; there was no electricity, she used oil lamps, and there was an outside toilet. Well, that was nothing new, we had one in London, but this one was a long way down the end of her garden. But

Pupils from Kings School, Rochester, evacuated to Lamberhurst, visit Bayham Abbey, June 1940. (Kent Messenger Newspaper Group)

she did keep the place very clean.' Audrey Wines recalls bath-time: 'We bathed in a saucer bath. It was like a big saucer, about eight inches deep, with a lip round the edge. There was an outside toilet with a wooden seat with three holes cut in it; if someone else came in when you were using it, you shared!' And June Cohen had a surprise one night: 'I woke up that night and saw the farmer sitting on a sort of chair – the next day I realised it was a commode!'

Sir Cecil Weir, Civil Defence Commissioner for the Western District of Scotland, made these observations: 'Some of the children came from slums where sanitary and washing conveniences were remarkable by their absence and many, and pathetic, were the stories told about the introduction of such little guests to entirely different environments.' Many stories portrayed children, never having seen a bath before, fearing they were to be drowned. Some were terrified of clean sheets – their families had never used them for sleeping in, only laying over dead bodies.

One headmistress from Chepstow, wrote the following in a report to Mass Observation:

The difficulty seems to be that many of the children have never learnt the ordinary decencies of life. What can be done with a child who picks up a

Instinctively Tommy drew closer to Sally, and their hands met and clasped.

" One of you dropped blackberry juice over my nice clean covers."

An illustration of evacuees 'from the poorer area' from a Woman's Weekly *story, December 1939; evacuees were still being glamorised.*

newspaper and goes into the corner of the drawing room instead of the lavatory?

Tales of the manner in which the children take their food are rife. Some of them will not sit at a table, but want to sit on the floor and have the food handed to them. This must be where there is overcrowding and there has been no room at the table. Some do not know how to use a knife and fork, they only use a knife. Others have never been used to sanitation, and foul the paths and gardens.

One boy said he never went to sleep lying down, he perched himself by the bedpost and went to bed clinging with his head resting on it. There had never been room in the bed for him to lie down. A little girl said she always went to bed in her frock and did not know what a nightgown was. I have read several reports of children, on arrival, going to bed and 'disappearing', only to be found later sleeping under the bed – at home they slept under their parents' bed.

Their clothes, or lack of them, was another cause of shock. Joan Rands remembers that: 'They (twin girls) were about my age, seven or eight years old, and they wet the beds to start with. The only clothes they had with them was a paper bag full of clean white ankle socks. Grandma called and asked mummy to let her have some of my sister's and my clothes for the twins.' Many poorer children were sewn into their underwear, which was changed in spring and autumn.

Many of those in the reception areas were shocked at the state of the children who arrived in their villages. The long train journey did not help – many who had started out looking neat and clean arrived dirty, grumpy, and dishevelled. S.A. Yates recollects her arrival: 'We eventually arrived at Box station in the early evening. We got off our train and assembled our goods and chattels, which were a push-chair, a suitcase wedged across it, two army blankets on top and my brother on top of that.' The majority soon appeared to adapt to their surroundings, as a report by the Chief Inspector for Elementary Schools of the Board of Education shows:

> The general picture of education in the reception areas is encouraging rather than discouraging. . . . There can be no doubt that many children's lives have been greatly enriched by their removal from large towns and, in the case of children from the worst homes, the conditions that make for sound education have been substantially improved. . . . The new interests and the wider basis of first-hand experience which the children have been getting might, on any broad view of education be felt to compensate for some falling-off in formal attainments.

Many tried to look at the positive aspects; the leader-writer of the *Surrey Advertiser* wrote: 'The Cockney adaptability and talent for rising to the occasion has repaid in laughter and friendliness any inconvenience householders may have suffered through billeting. The mental picture of "Little London hooligans" has been pleasantly disillusioned.' And humour there often was. Donald Wood remembers: 'We had two boys billeted with us, Bobby Ovett, about six, and Raymond Watkins, about eight, from Battersea. Dad was out when the boys arrived. As he came in the front door later, he was greeted by Bobby who said, "Wotcher, mister – you the bloke what lives upstairs?" – smiles all round, an innocent remark which told us plenty.'

Humorous though they now seem, these issues could not be overlooked. It was admitted in 1941 that there had been grave fears from the start that problems of lice and dirty habits in many of the children from slum areas might sabotage the whole evacuation exercise, and could even introduce disease and epidemics into the countryside. As early as 15 September 1939, a *Times* leader commented: 'The insanitary cases, verminous or diseased, must be treated at once as infringements of the public health requirements and be subjected to medical and judicious disciplinary treatment. The Ministry of Health acknowledges that the billeting of this type of person in respectable homes is unreasonable.' Head lice were a particular problem. The WVS produced leaflets on the condition for distribution

Evacuees Bobby Ovett (left) and Raymond Watkins (right), from Battersea, with billeters' son Donald Woods (centre) and Chummy the dog, September 1939.

among housewives in the reception areas. The book *Ourselves in Wartime* contains the following story about an evacuated primary school:

> A young WVS volunteer walked in to see if she could help. The Head Teacher greeted her with no small measure of relief, and calling the children handed them over to her, together with a cake of antiseptic soap, and the apparently simple words "you can do their hair." The significance of 'doing their hair' as against 'washing their hair' was yet to dawn on the girl. The children enlightened her. "We got nits, we 'ave" a curly-haired youngster announced; and the other twenty-three echoed proudly, "We got nits."

Lavender Clarke describes her evacuees: 'They were from Bethnal Green; when they arrived they were full of nits – mother nearly had kittens. She spent hours combing them out.'

The journey and often cramped conditions in the billets and temporary schools meant that contagious diseases took their toll. Margaret Cronin remembers a serious outbreak of diphtheria among evacuees at the end of 1939: 'There were children from all over, and they put us all in a big hall. They tested us all to find the carriers and then inoculated us; several of the children died.' Mary Noyle remembers being ill:

I caught diphtheria and was wrapped in a bright red woollen blanket (which was very scratchy) and taken in an ambulance to the fever hospital on the Totnes Road, opposite the cemetery! I can remember being two in a bed, one at the top and one at the bottom, in a boys' ward with a screen around us. Later I was moved to the girls' ward, still two in a bed. No visitors were allowed, but they could see us in bed by standing on a high bank just outside the windows. I spent my eighth birthday there, I can only remember having Bovril to drink and a Rowntree's fruit gum which my mother had thrown in the window.

Most of the problems were of a more mundane, if unpleasant character. Betty Jones explained that: 'I got impetigo and ended up being sent to the isolation hospital. Aunty, the lady I lived with, used to cycle out to visit me.' Bryan Farmer recalled how: 'Some were infected with ringworm and had to have their heads shaved and painted with iodine, which made them objects of ridicule among the natives who had never seen anything like it.' Fred Bond from Guernsey recounts one ironic incidence: 'On arriving at my relatives' house, I was informed that my wife and daughter were safe in Glasgow. At last I began to smile again, because we had spent days escaping the imminent German invasion of Guernsey, only to learn that my daughter and other children in Glasgow had contracted GERMAN MEASLES!'

London evacuees in a Devonshire fishing village.

Another dreadful problem was the number of evacuee children killed on the roads. It was felt that one of the major reasons for this was that some of the foster-parents had not had children of their own, and did not understand the dangers 'of, for example, sending young children without a companion on errands which entail crossing a busy road, or of allowing them to play in streets open to traffic.' Maureen Phizacklea from Suffolk remembers one sad accident: 'My sister's London friend Mavis was unfortunately knocked off her bicycle and died and was buried in Brundish churchyard – her young brother stayed in London and was safe!' Billeting officers were instructed to warn foster parents of these dangers.

Not all the evacuees were from the working classes. A fair number were from middle-class suburbs and for some of them the differences were just as great. Christine Jones comments:

> The destination for our smallish group was Duckinfield in Cheshire, and what a cultural shock it proved to be. We left a leafy suburb of clean semi's in roads called Ash, Poplar, Beech, etc., to be confronted with tall blackened chimneys, cobbled streets and narrow roads of terraced houses, because Duckinfield was, of course, a cotton mill town on the borders of Lancashire. It proved to be quite an eye-opener; you can imagine what it was like for a ten-year-old to see for the first time people with clogs, 'knocker uppers', shopping baskets always covered with white cloths to protect the bread etc. from 'smuts', Lancashire hot-pot, and 'socials' where the refreshments included peas on a saucer covered with vinegar.'

Joyce Fry also experienced some shocks: 'We were then taken to a back-to-back house, with no toilet or bath. Six houses shared the keys to two toilets at the end of the road. There was a rota in the street for a bath once a week.'

As is clear from the stories recounted above, the troubles were far from being one-sided. Christine Pilgrim from Peckham witnessed prejudice as an evacuee:

> The people there always assumed that because you came from east London you'd never seen a bath before. I came across prejudice for the first time then – we were always referred to as 'bloody vackees'. My sister won a scholarship while we were there, it was the first the village school had had for some years – the pupils all had a half-day on the strength of it – but the adults were awful about it. 'What a shocking waste of a scholarship on a bloody vackee' – just like some people said about black children in the 1950s.

Christine's point about the parallels between the evacuees and postwar immigrants is very true, as many of the criticisms and problems experienced by the evacuees were shared by the immigrants just a few years later. Walter Hurst recalls similar resentment: 'The locals were very suspicious of us and felt we were being advantaged at their expense, for example, taking places at the Grammar School when we passed the 11 plus. However, in the main, I can only praise the local folk in taking us in and giving us good homes for such a long time.' This feeling of unequal treatment was widespread, as this extract from *William and the Evacuees*, published in 1940, demonstrates:

The original caption tells us that 'Here are some of a party of forty children from London and Gravesend, all under six, evacuated to Devon'. (HMSO)

'We want to be 'vacuated too,' said Arabella Simpkin, a red-haired long-nosed girl, who automatically constituted herself the leader of any group of which she formed part. 'They get all the fun . . .'

'Yes,' grumbled Frankie Miller, a small, stout, snub-nosed boy of seven. 'They got a Christmas party an' a Christmas tree.'

'An' tins of sweets all round,' put in Ella Poppleham, a morose-looking child, with a shock of black hair and a squint. 'A whole tin of sweets each. It's not fair, it isn't. Puttin' on side an' havin' parties an' eatin' whole tins of sweets. It's not fair. We oughter be 'vacuated, too.'

'I been 'vacuated," said a small, foursquare child proudly. 'It made my arm come up somethin' korful.'

Sometimes the locals had good reason to complain. Lillian Clegg confessed that: 'We woke up the village of Grafton, roaming the roads at night singing "South of the Border", and "Harbour Lights".' Bryan Farmer remembers: 'The boy who shared my desk was called Bailey, a ginger-haired, spotty-faced, snotty-nosed, aggressive kid who elbowed, pinched and punched me throughout the day, establishing his authority with whispered threats of what he would do to me after school, using words quite foreign to me, whom he called a "swede-bashing bastard".' On the whole this mutual hostility soon faded and a, sometimes uneasy, truce prevailed. Eddie Roland commented how: 'In Leeds we were accepted as part of the community. There was a war on, constant air raids – people had more to think about than some evacuees.'

In matching over a million evacuees with billets in such a small time, it was inevitable that some matches would prove disastrous, but the problems were deeply compounded by these cultural and social differences, and by the natural homesickness of children, many of whom were away from home for the first time. Letters began to appear in *The Times*; commenting on a debate in Parliament in October 1939, the paper said:

> It is not surprising that the House of Commons was impelled last night to discuss the problems of evacuation. Certain troubles and grievances were bound to follow the dispersal of nearly a million and a half town-dwellers, mostly children and women, into the country and other areas of safety. None of the complaints put forward in our correspondence columns has been trivial or unreasonable. Collectively, however, they are serious, and are even more widespread than the published letters have indicated. The Ministries of Health and Education have, in communications to local authorities, recognised the necessity for remedial measures, and are stirring up the authorities to helpful and sympathetic action, and assuring them of Treasury assistance.

The different social classes were forced to look at each other at close range, and the middle classes were appalled by what they saw. The demand for change was loud and widespread. Sir Cecil Weir commented that: 'This evacuation has probably done quite a lot to break down class prejudice, but the building of decent homes will do much more. It is the key to the social revolution of progress we all want to bring about.' In 1941 the Government asked a committee chaired by Sir William Beveridge, a well-known economist and ex-director of the London School of Economics, to advise them on how to introduce a system of 'social security'. The Beveridge Committee's Report was published in December 1942, and debated in Parliament in February 1943 with the government accepting most of its main points, the report became the basis of the Welfare State and the National Health Service.

Slowly, however, the evacuees settled in, as Jane Black recalls: 'At first the girls were not very keen on staying, they didn't like the country. But they soon got used to it, they loved the animals and especially the food. We had better food than in the city, of course, being in the country.' George Powis remembers his billet family: 'Mr and Mrs Oram's house was a modern semi with a bathroom and toilets – heaven to us inner-city lads who had never seen this. They also had a garden and Mrs Oram's sister had an orchard, chickens and pigs. In the phoney war some lads went back to Brum but I was very, very happy and it never entered my head to go home.' Those who stayed began to enjoy country life as they learnt more about it, as Betty Jones explains: 'When we first got there they were harvesting so we went out into the fields and helped. They had apple trees in the house where I was. I remember helping to pick the apples and pack them. I can also recall making rush baskets out of the reeds – just for fun.' Roy Judge has similar memories: 'I helped to pick the apples, there were several different types, and we stored them in hay in an outside storehouse. There was a bit of a lawn that I had the job of mowing.' Eric Sephton recalls: '. . . Peter being chased by a

'Vacuation' cards – the Evacuees. 'Betty Butter', with her flowers, shows the 'classic city kid in the country' scene, and 'Johnny Jinks' speaks for himself.

turkey. There was a battered old car behind the shed, and my sister had a ride on a pig. My greatest memories are the long summer days, a million miles from the war, and that farmyard smell.' David Wood helped on the farm: 'We did little jobs around the farm, collecting the chickens eggs, feeding the chickens, helping with the harvest and haymaking,' and Iris McCartney remembers the jobs she used to do too:

> She used to have an allotment; we used to help her on it, digging up potatoes and beans, and helping her preserve stuff. I also used to go and help with the horses in the stables nearby – I enjoyed that. Me and my friend used to cycle to Moreton in the Marsh, about four miles, to go to the cinema, twice a week if there was something good on. In the summer we used to go to a place called Lower Swell and build up the banks of the brook so we could swim in it.

Mr L. Powis describes his experiences: 'Most of us were real "townies" and the countryside was more like some foreign country. We learned hop-picking and served as beaters for the pheasant shoots which we really enjoyed; all the men wore breeches and gaiters, which we never saw in the city. I and a couple of others were billeted in the house of Mr Hopkins, the estate agent, who used to organise

Young evacuees on a farm cart. There were many photographs in the press showing urban children enjoying the countryside.

Evacuees, Luton, 1939. The girl on the left is Clara, a kindertransport refugee from Germany, the girl in the centre is the householder's daughter, and on the right is June Wolfson, née Cohen.

the shoots for the guests of Colonel Hopton, the local landowner.' Frances Hardy from Birkenhead was given a special task:

It was decided that I should be the kitchen maid and I was soon put to the task of preparing vegetables every evening for the following day's meal. My other Saturday tasks included cleaning all the silver once a fortnight and cleaning several pairs of boots. If there was any time left after all my chores I was allowed to go out and play.

Harvest time was a big event, everyone was involved. Even children had their job to do. When the old haystack was being cleared out and prepared for the next crop, all hands were required, even the children. All I was expected to do was to bash mice and rats on the head with a big stick. These frantic animals would flee from the remains of the hayrick while all and sundry stood around waiting with their weapons.

A distinctly more pleasurable part of harvest time was the actual work in the fields. As children we would carry the heavy basket of goodies, accompanied by countless bottles of cider. I couldn't help wondering why everyone was so jolly!

Of course, billets weren't all in the country. Roy Simon stayed in a town: 'Paddock Head seemed to be an exciting place to us youngsters. I had lots of friends, we were always out and about, scouring the shops for comics, then swapping them with each other. There always seemed to be lots going on. Stan and I always had lots to do after school, weekends and holidays. We also loved the cinema and went with my parents about four times a week.'

Even in the country, the cinema was the most popular of entertainments: Betty Goodyear describes her billet: 'They also owned the local cinema [in Pontnewydd] which was next door to the house and my sister and I were allowed to see each programme once, which meant at least two visits each week, free. Then we lay in bed at night we could hear the sound from the cinema next door and once we had seen the film we knew what was happening, so this kept us entertained too.' Eddie Roland also remembers a trip to the cinema: 'I'll never forget the night we decided to visit the cinema and see a Deanna Durbin film. She had a lovely voice, but when she sang "Beneath the Lights of Home" all around us in the darkened cinema, women started to cry.'

In January 1941 the Shakespeare Committee on conditions in the reception areas found that in the great majority of cases evacuation was succeeding. Some months later the Minister of Health stated that 80 per cent of the movement on the reception side had been a success. But any exercise on that scale was bound to have some failures, albeit only a small percentage. Some billets were just plainly unsuitable, as Jean Garnham comments: 'There were all these single men who

Evacuees in Bridgend, Glamorgan, summer 1941. The little girl standing right front is June Wolfson, née Cohen.

had evacuees billeted with them – they wouldn't dream of doing it today.' Christine Pring described how:

> We were re-housed, this time, to the "other" part of Duckinfield, narrow back-to-back houses, and to a young mother, no more than nineteen, whose husband was in the army. The house was in a very poor state; orange boxes for a cupboard, and very worn, hand-me-down furniture, sadly, not very clean. In her defence, the young girl was hardly able to look after herself and her baby, and to expect her to be able to control a ten- and twelve-year-old was asking too much. I expect we began to look rather unkempt, and if something came up we did not go to school.
>
> One day we decided to take the baby to see Alice and Frank, so we scrubbed up the old pram, cleaned and tidied the baby and set forth. Up we went to the bedroom where poor Alice was still unwell. I remember her being pleased to see us but crying – what a motley crew we must have looked. Little did we know that Alice was so shocked she telegrammed my mother. My mother arrived the next day to take us home – on reflection I think the authorities had let us down.'

Iris Gent endured a number of billets: 'The fourth place I went to, the lady was in what you could only call an advanced stage of senility; she never went up to bed, she sat up all night and talked to herself. We ran the place, we made the meals and had our boyfriends back. Then her nieces came to visit – they were horrified – they went to see the billeting officer and told her she couldn't possibly look after any evacuees, so we were moved again.'

In other places life was made miserable by cold 'foster parents'. Christine Pring describes her situation:

> 'My' Alice was not a maternal person, and made it very clear that the house was to be kept neat and tidy at all times, so cushions were plumped, beds made virtually as you stepped out and, as she worked, tea made ready for her return. However, I was quite an amenable child and fell in with this regime quite easily. It was, however, made perfectly clear that her having me was an act of kindness and certainly no mention was made of the payments my parents made and the fact that they were billed for any extras. There were small unkindnesses that took place which I felt very deeply.

Margaret Cronin experienced some hostility too: 'I was billeted with a Welsh family in a small terraced house. He was nice, but she kept making snide remarks like "people from London are all dirty". We used to have to get up early on Saturday mornings and go to the market; we each had a list and had to join a different queue.' Walter Hurst missed his family: 'One thing that sticks out above all else was the constant desire that someone should put their arms around me and tell me I was loved.'

Sometimes it seemed that the evacuees were taken on purely for monetary gain. Alice Morgan felt this:

I think they only wanted the money; we were not allowed to stop in, we had to walk the streets, even in the snow – we both had terrible chilblains. On Saturday she sent us to queue for a pound of sausages each; we was that hungry on the way home we used to eat one raw. The only time we had a cooked meal was when my mum and dad came to see us; the rest of the time we had bread and jam. My brother, who was in the Navy, sent us a big box of goodies from America; they opened it before we saw it and took a pile of things out. My sister broke a sugar basin and they wrote and told my mother that she had done something wicked and my Mum had to pay for it. My brother Jack who was in the RAF read between the lines of the letters I wrote to him – he said to Mum that he thought we wasn't happy or being treated right, so he said if you don't fetch them home I will. He came with his wife to fetch us home, and I looked that thin he couldn't believe it.

Evacuees Phyllis Wilkins (centre), aged eight, and her sister Vera, aged thirteen, with their mother, Gloucester, April 1941.

Roy Simon had to work hard for his family:

Billy Osbourne and I were dispatched to a farm in Cheshire. My time spent on that farm is etched on my mind as being very tough and unhappy. Billy and I had to work like Trojans, we both had our regular jobs as well as anything that came along. Pigsties, animals, land work, we were like farm workers only not so well treated. Dad had found out where I was, he was really shocked when he saw my dirty and unkempt appearance. He started berating the farmer and his wife, but they more or less told him to clear off – we were billeted with them, and Billy and I were jolly well going to stay and work on the farm. Anyway, Dad produced proof of 'ownership' and I was on my way. Unhappily, Dad didn't have any papers for Billy, and we had to leave him there. The sight of Billy's stricken face and hearing him cry hysterically as we left will stay with me forever. Dad did his best, I cried and he pleaded with the farmer, but to no avail.

Archie Salvidge from Bermondsey laboured hard too: 'There was no money then. I worked on the farms around Ashton – no schooling – I worked very hard all day in all weathers to earn eightpence an hour – slave labour – I remember having to hide from the school board man!'

Some of the older children took matters into their own hands. Iris Gent recalls that: 'My friend Harold was in so many unfortunate places; he had little to eat,

A visit by the Mayor of Hull to Lincolnshire, September 1941. The mayor is seen here with babies delivered to evacuated Hull mothers. (Hull Central Library)

and he was six foot and still growing! He got a tent which he pitched in the fields to live in, but people took his things, so he and a friend moved into a garage. I remember them cooking on a spirit stove.'

The authorities were not blind to the problems and attempts were made, not always successfully, to combat the worst excesses. In *Croydon and the Second World War* it is recorded that:

> By the end of the year [1939] eleven care committees, consisting of the billeting officer, head teachers for each kind of school and a number of helpers, were working. They visited the mothers and children, advising on the problems arising in their billets, putting them into touch with medical, social, and amusement facilities; arranged for cheap milk; for a minor ailments clinic for children under five; for hot dinners for the little ones at three pence per head; for small homes to take them when their mothers were in hospital and for other homes for children unsuitable for private billeting. Nursery classes, with laundry facilities and needlework assistance were provided for the mothers.

In June 1940 welfare committees were set up in reception areas; the LCC seconded children's care organisers to regional offices to coordinate their work, and organisers were sent to help local education and billeting authorities. This proved so successful that many other authorities followed suit. Schemes arising from this included the London Clothing Scheme set up in November 1940. Clothing depots, run by the WVS and coordinated by the LCC, were set up in the reception areas for the supply of clothing to unaccompanied children. The clothes were made up of 'official' and 'gift' supplies, the gifts being largely supplied by the American Red Cross. Parents were means-tested and, based on this, paid a proportion of the costs. Parties of mothers in some cases formed working parties and mended the children's clothes and socks.

Throughout the war, close communications were kept between the home authorities and the reception authorities as to the health, education and welfare of the evacuees. The Medical Officer of Health in the sending area kept in contact with the Medical Officer of Health in the receiving areas, so that they could keep track of the health and treatment of the evacuated children. It was recommended that reception areas set up Welfare Committees 'as a means of planning assistance to householders and evacuated persons and in order that all welfare problems, whether concerned with unaccompanied children or other evacuated persons, may receive careful consideration.' It was recommended that committees include

Secondary schoolboys from London, evacuated to Wales, do PT on the beach. (Crown Copyright)

representatives of the billeting authority, the sending authority (e.g. teachers or helpers) and voluntary organisations.

School

The children arrived at their new homes in the summer holidays, and because of the difficulties in finding suitable buildings, equipment, books, etc., the holiday tended to stretch on. Slowly, however, schooling began to start again. Buildings were the greatest problem, often a double shift system with the local school was introduced, but in that late summer of '39, when the weather was still good, many lessons took place in the fields or on beaches, adding to the feeling that it was all a great adventure. Teachers went round the billets at night to see the children were in bed in good time.

Margaret Woodrow was a teacher with an evacuated school. She gives a vivid account of the problems of setting up:

> There was no room at the local school and my classroom was to be in the Village Hall, a wood and corrugated iron building with a stove heater which smoked when the wind was in a certain direction. I had the nine- to thirteen-year-olds, and another teacher who was used to infants had the younger group.

A visit by the Mayor of Hull, Councillor Sydney Smith, to Hull evacuees at Hatfield Modern School, September 1941; subjects taught included bee-keeping. (Hull Central Library)

Boys from Kings School, Rochester, were evacuated to Lamberhurst. Parts of Scotney Castle were used for classrooms, seen here in June 1940. (Kent Messenger Newspaper Group)

At first we had to manage with just rough note books and pencils. On the good side, outside work was a new experience, the beautiful area and fresh, clean air and nature walks with wild flower collecting, mounting seaweed collections, painting on the cliffs and in lovely gardens, visiting farms for potato planting and milking cows.

I was twenty one and was thrown in at the deep end with many responsibilities; visiting billets, handling complaints, writing for help with clothing, staying on hand during Christmas holidays, etc., and making up lessons for such a mixed group. The sole lavatory was a bench seat with a hole in it and a bucket underneath, in a shed like a sentry box outside the building. A senior pupil would stand guard when the teacher used it. I made so many requests for toilets that I felt, if Queen Mary [Tudor] had 'Calais' written on her heart, then 'Lavatories' would be written on mine.

We brought sandwiches for lunch, and made Oxo drinks with hot water from an urn in a tiny kitchen. We found a set of booklets in a cupboard belonging to one of the groups that used the hall. They contained the music for three hymns; I managed to play them in turn for Morning Prayers – I have disliked 'He who would valiant be' ever since.

Some children returned home and the numbers in our village stabilised, when evacuee numbers dropped some local ten-year-olds joined us. Thirty to

Penard Church Hall, South Wales, 1941. This was typical of the sorts of buildings used as temporary evacuee schools.

forty boxes of equipment arrived, and we had a library box which was exchanged from time to time with the local library. The headmaster of the village school called occasionally to see how we were managing, The hall was still used for village affairs during the evenings and I was pleased to attend the weekly dances.

Archie Salvidge remembers taking his lunch to school too: 'We used to bring spuds to school, where we were allowed to cook them on a black stove in the middle of the classroom.'

Suitable buildings were hard to find, as Frances Hardy explains: 'The evacuees were distributed between two schools. The first ones to arrive were absorbed into the village school, but the later arrivals, of whom I was one, were schooled separately a little further along the village in the very small rooms which formed part of the British Legion Hall.' Miriam McLeod remembers sharing a school building:

We shared the school building with the local school. We used it in the morning and used the Working Man's Institute in the afternoon. On the first day there were about fifty or sixty children sitting on the floor, waiting for our teacher to arrive. It was so grim, there were nets on the windows and we didn't know each other; I panicked and went back to my billet. It was a wet day and I took off my wellingtons and stepped in the puddles so I could say I came home because my feet were wet.

Walter Hurst also had to share school facilities: 'At first, school was sharing with local children, then we got use of the Memorial Hall, where we had four classes – one in each corner. The teachers performed miracles with very little help in the way of books and materials, and I think we thrived in spite of the difficulties. We leaned much about nature and wild life and enjoyed fresh air and good plain food. Nature study lessons were common.' Iris McCartney enjoyed the nature studies too: 'We used to collect rose hips for syrup, you'd take them to school where they'd weigh them, we used to get paid a little bit for that. We used to study the wild flowers and the birds and do a report on them at school.'

Public schools fared no better and often shared premises too, as Philip D'Arthreau remembers:

I was evacuated along with fourteen other pupils from my school, Victoria College, by mailboat on June 21st 1940. The headmaster had decided that those of us preparing to take our public examinations should go to England in order to complete them. We arrived at Shrewsbury School where we stayed for a term. At the end of the term we were transferred to Bedford School, by now the headmaster had rounded up about thirty-six pupils from the school who

Evacuees sketching in Pobbles (?) bay, 1941.

Evacuees and woolly friends at Davis Farm, 1941.

had been evacuated to Britain, and we moved in as a separate school, keeping our own uniforms. I left the school in 1943, having gained entry to Cambridge University.

It was at school, of course, that the evacuated children met most of the peers with whom they would share the next few years. As happens with children, relationships, to begin with at least, were not always easy. Phyllis Wilkins remembers: 'The local children could be very hurtful. They used to taunt us, "You're from London – You're an evacuee", that sort of thing.' Kathleen Corton remembers similar, if perhaps more amusing, insults: 'There was some mickey-taking from the village children, they used to call us Londoners – they used it as an insult – and say things like, "all you eat is fish and chips", we used to give them back as good as we got, but there was never any viciousness.' Miriam McLeod has mixed memories: 'The lady was very nice, but she had a son about my age who was very spoilt, he threw things at us and things like that; she asked us not to mention it to my mother.' David Wood had a similar experience: 'I went to the village school, it was a big Victorian house which had been converted. There was one other evacuee boy with me. Most of the local kids were alright, but there was one boy who was a bit of a bully, called Bertie. There was no fisticuffs, just abuse, he used to call us "townies", "Londoners", stuff like that.'

And this sort of thing wasn't confined to Londoners. Betty Collas from Jersey came up against it too: 'Mostly I thoroughly enjoyed my schooling. There was a bit of bullying – name-calling. They knew we had French connections – one little girl asked if I had blue blood – I was worried as she was standing with a pin in her hand!' Indeed, the Channel Islands children often came in for particularly harsh treatment. Roy Simon from Guernsey remembers: 'At school we were teased because of our strange accent. We were called foreigners and picked on in a big way as children do.' Eddie Roland found much the same: 'At first we used to try and explain that we were British, flew the British flag, and spoke mainly English. My cousin and I used to get into fights because of name-calling and after one skirmish we were taken in front of the headmaster, Mr Holt. He believed in fair play and after hearing about the local difficulties, said he would have no more of this rumpus and thereafter peace reigned.' Fighting often broke out among the boys, as John Kirk recalls: 'At the school everyone asked, "Can I bash you?" I said, "You can try if you like."' Archie Salvidge from Bermondsey recollects similar playground hostility: 'We started our first school under a Cornish teacher, Mr Edwards, which did not work out as there were lots of fights between the London and Cornish kids.'

But children being children, most soon settled down and made friends. Rozel Garnier remembers that: 'I went to Dalmain Road School. I got on well with the other kids – they'd never heard of Jersey, they asked questions, how do you get there? do you walk? bus? bicycle?' The schools tried to help, as Betty Gagg

Girls from Chatham County School during a dance lesson in a temporary classroom. (Kent Messenger *Newspaper Group*)

Girls' school evacuees in a drama production.
(Southwark Local History Unit)

explains: 'At school we were each allocated an evacuee to show round the school and village. Mine was Jean Slade from Sidcup.' Joan Stephenson recalls how: 'We put up six boys who had been evacuated from Brockley Central School. We used to get on very well. I got on especially well with a couple of brothers, John and David. We had a lot of fun, we used to do dares, and they used to teach me a bit of their French they learnt at school.' Kenneth Dobson also made friends: 'I got on very well with all the kids there. The first year I invited all the kids to my birthday party – mum was running around the street asking all the women if they'd got any jellies to lend her. There were a lot of evacuees there from Guernsey and Jersey, and a Jewish boy from somewhere in Europe. Everybody accepted everyone else because there was a war on.' Pamela Buckley also has some happy memories: 'During the five years we made friends, and for me one very special friend, a "Bury lass" who lived opposite me. We went to school together and felt oh so sad to have to part in September 1945.' There were even, of course, romances, as Ernie Prowse from Stoke-in-Teignhead, remembers:

I was very lucky to meet an evacuee at a dance in Shaldon. She was sixteen and a half when I first met her, she and her mum had come down to live there as the bombing had got worse in London. I was lucky to meet such a pretty girl as it was the first time her mum had let her come to the dance with the girl next door. I took her home afterwards – I kissed her goodnight and she fainted in my arms and I had to knock on the door, so it was not a very good start. They took her indoors and I was off up the road back to Stoke feeling a bit doubtful what I would do next. So, I picked a nice bunch of anemones for Iris and a nice cauliflower for her mother, and it was all OK. I got my feet under the table, so we courted for three years and we have been married for fifty-four very happy years.

As usual, teachers, good and bad, stick in the minds of the pupils. Mr S.A. Yates remembers Miss Burton: 'I settled into village life, learnt to read under the formidable and terrifying Miss Burton who used to scare me to death! I remember standing in line, desperately trying to follow the text of the reading book until it was my turn, dreading the inevitable mistake or hesitation that

Hull evacuees at Hatfield Modern School meet the mayor and mayoress in September 1941.
(Hull Central Library)

would result in a savage yank of the hair just above my right ear.' Eddie Roland has his own memories of one particular teacher:

I had started school again, this time at Great Horton School. I was not happy there. There was a particular schoolmaster, Mr Sykes, who made my life very difficult. He would shout loudly and humiliate me often. He realised fairly quickly that this wasn't working, so resorted to hitting me about the head several times a day. It was the last straw for Mr Sykes and for me – I started to play truant.

Many local newspapers in the evacuation areas kept in close contact with the evacuees from their area, either through the schools or through the local paper in the reception area, and ran regular items under headings such as 'Evacuation News', reporting on such things as the school sports days, etc. One item which appeared in the *Kentish Mercury* of February 1942, announced that:

THEY SANG BETTER THAN THE WELSH – Deptford Children's Eisteddfod Successes. Evacuated pupils of Creek Road Senior Boys' and Senior Girls'

The Mayor of Hull with evacuees in a classroom at Hatfield Modern School, September, 1941. (Hull Central Library)

School took part in an Eisteddfod held in Blaenau Village, in Carmarthenshire, with considerable success a few days ago. The competitors were drawn from quite a large area . . . to compete in singing, recitation and written competition. The Deptford children obtained more awards than the Welsh people themselves.

The article also demonstrates how schools threw themselves into the life of the local communities. Betty Robinson remembers: 'There was a college in Shebbear and on one occasion they put on a play for our school, so we thought we would do a show for them. My friend Enez and me were Gert and Daisy. We cut out funny bits from the comics, then we sang, 'My sister and I'. I did a solo, "In my sweet little alice-blue gown", but I forgot the words.' Teachers frequently took part in village life as organists or choirmasters, trainers of football and netball teams and concert organisers.

Subsequent evacuations and re-evacuations were of a far more piecemeal nature than the first. The process of evacuating a school, together with its entire staff and all its pupils, was no longer feasible on the whole, and children moving into reception areas joined the local school, or even a school previously evacuated. Some parties were merged together to form entirely new schools. Added to this, there was a steady fall in school rolls because of the drift back, and consequently some schools were forced to close, and their remaining pupils absorbed into the local schools. Two years after the war started, half of all London elementary schoolchildren in the reception areas were in merged or local schools, the secondary figure was somewhat less.

In October 1939 the Home Secretary announced that the Government no longer considered the carrying of gas masks to be necessary in the reception areas.

Hull evacuees at Hatfield Modern School, September 1941; subjects taught included domestic science. (Hull Central Library)

However, evacuees were not completely cut off from the war. Margaret Cronin remembers: 'Later, when the Battle of Britain started, the dog-fights became our entertainment; we used to sit on a five-bar-gate and watch them.' Phyllis Wilkins recalls a close encounter with the enemy: 'One time my aunt was pegging out the washing, I was in the garden with her. A German plane, a Messerschmitt I think you call it, came down. My aunt froze. "Get behind me" she said. We were waiting for him to fire, but he didn't – he just waved at us.' David Wood explained how: 'Mum and Dad privately arranged for me to go back to the farm. We weren't blitzed there, of course, but one day after a raid on Bristol one of the planes dropped two bombs in one of the fields. I suppose he jettisoned them.' June Cohen did not avoid the raids either: 'My mother took us to relatives in Glasgow, but there were raids there too; we slept in the Underground. My mother used to take a full hot-water bottle down with us. The next day, when you came out, the water had sometimes been cut off by the bombs, but you could boil the water in the bottle.'

Evacuees from Southwark Central School for Girls enjoy 'winter sports', 1939. (Southwark Local History Unit)

Christmas

With all the shortages, war-time Christmases were often low-key, but most people did their best. Betty Collas, evacuated to Surrey remembers: 'lovely Christmases; we played lots of games. There was one with three vases of holly, you had to step over them – blindfolded! As soon as you were blindfolded, the vases were taken away. This was the time of rationing so there were few presents. I remember one year I received some red knitting yarn, not wool, and a pair of knitting needles.' Phyllis Wilkins was evacuated to Gloucestershire and also recalls there being just a few presents: 'I remember Christmas in Westbury-upon-Severn, I made a doll out of some old stuff. We had a stocking, we got an apple and a few bits of whatever we could get.' Mavis Kerr spent Christmas in Devon: 'At Christmas there would be a round of going to late suppers to relatives, after milking; this went on until the beginning of February.' Walter Hurst was in Wales: 'Christmas was very much a non-event. I really cannot remember much celebration – certainly no turkey.' Peggy Masterson was a billeter from Suffolk: 'I remember one Christmas, I was eleven or twelve. Mr Sanders used to come sometimes and stay for the weekend; he came to stay that Christmas. He'd made little cots and Mrs Sanders had made the bedclothes, and there was a doll in each; there were three of them – one for each of the girls and one for me!' Joyce Fry, evacuated to Somerset, remembers making presents too: 'At Christmas the girls had to knit a present for Mum. It was in the shape of an orange carrot. We then had to fill it with mothballs – the poor postman!' Joyce Withers, evacuated to Cheshire, remembers:

'The Southwark Central Puppet Guild'. Evacuees from Southwark Central Girls' School perform a marionette show. (Southwark Local History Unit)

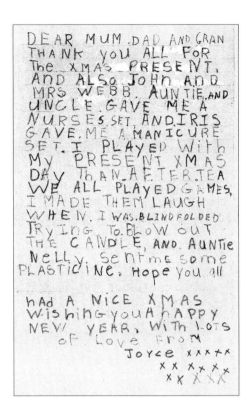

A Christmas letter from evacuee Joyce Fry.
'Auntie and Uncle' are her foster parents.

I was billeted with a Mr and Mrs Norbury. I spent a Christmas with them, which to me was the most memorable one ever as a child. I was told I should write a letter to Santa Claus, I did, ever mindful that there was 'a war on' and toys were scarce. Under supervision, my letter was sent up the chimney, I knew then that Santa Claus would receive it! Christmas morning finally came. I woke early, and there at the bottom of my bed was a pillow case full to the brim with presents. I couldn't believe my eyes, never before had I received so many presents, and especially not in a pillow case! I then decided I couldn't be so lucky, perhaps they were not all for me – so I waited for Mr and Mrs Norbury to come to my room. They were not long in doing so and stated the presents were all mine, then they stayed with me while I unpacked them. I was so happy and what a great Christmas that was.

Margaret Cordell recalls Christmas at Waddesdon Manor in Berkshire: 'At Christmas, a female member of staff dressed up as Father Christmas and we had a Nativity play. I sang "Silent Night" and "O, Willow Tree", and Mr and Mrs Rothschild sat and watched it all.'

In some areas parties were laid on. In 1939 £15,000 was raised by various sources, such as newspapers, to entertain evacuees at Christmas. Later, voluntary contributions were supplemented by 1s. per child paid from the rates of the

Southwark evacuees at a Christmas party in Worthing. (Courtesy of the Worthing Herald)

receiving authorities. In 1940 John Fletcher, a retired commercial traveller from Bury, started a fund to provide Christmas presents for all the Channel Islands children in the town between the ages of three and fourteen, collecting donations from as far afield as Canada, the USA, Australia and New Zealand. Every child received a present worth at least 5*s*. – a fairly large sum then. He continued to do the same each Christmas until 1944, when shortages of available goods caused the work to stop. Pamela Nicolle remembers him: 'Every so often we would have clothes from Canada and every Christmas toys from Danemoore; Mr Fletcher was responsible for organising all of this and I felt ever so grateful to him for his hard work and kindness.'

NINE

Homecoming and After

In areas that missed the V-weapon assault, such as Birmingham, full-scale, official, permanent return, known as de-vacuation, began on 6 December 1944, with trains bringing home evacuees from Cardiff to Hollingbourne and from South Wales to Reading. While in the south of England, plans were completed in March 1945 for the organised return of official evacuees for whom accommodation was available.

In London eight dispersal points were set up for the returning evacuees, where preparations were made to feed them on arrival, and give them a warm welcome home. The return of the London evacuees, which was spread over four weeks, is described in *War on the Line*, the record of the Southern Railway:

> The train came in and instantly there sprang into action the stewards with their red armlets and the volunteer porters with violet ones. Every passenger on the train bore a label of destination, and in a wonderfully short time they were collected into groups along the platforms. Many of the children were incidentally so small that they must have been born in the country and this must have been their first sight of London. Everybody, down to the smallest child, was perfectly tranquil and unruffled. Now a gate was opened and one group after another marched down the platform and through the gate. 'Brown bus for mauve labels' announced a steward, and the bus was soon filled or not quite filled, since it seems that for one reason or another there are never so many travellers as have been expected. It cannot have been more than a quarter of an hour from the train's drawing in that the first bus passed out of the station and then another and another on its heels.

Most looked forward eagerly to their return, including Betty Collas:

> Our return home was greatly looked forward to. I frequently used to dream about going home and going to see my aunt and uncle and cousins – I was always so disappointed when I woke up.
>
> We were on one of the first boats back. It was actually very scary – a minesweeper went in front of our boat. It was wonderful when we got to St Helier, the whole pier was crowded with people who'd come to see if any of their friends or relatives were on the boat. In one way I was sad; I'd known the children in Godalming for three years and had made many good friends there.

Not all the children wanted to go home though. Some, like Mavis Kerr, wanted to stay: 'I didn't want to come back – my mother sent my sister, who was on leave from the WAAF, to pick me up. I created merry hell.' And sometimes it was not all that was expected, as Rozel Garnier remembers on her return to St Helier, Jersey: 'We managed to be allowed to go back in October 1944; we lost most of our luggage on the way back. I was thrilled to come back, although things were still bad, we had to have Red Cross parcels for a few weeks.' Enid Taylor returned to Guernsey: 'I remember it was pouring with rain, but we were back home after five years. When we went away our house was left with our belongings in; the Germans lived in them so you can imagine the mess they were in after five years. It wasn't fit to live in, so we lived with my grandmother.' A few – a very few – found their parents did not want them back. There was sadness too, as friends were parted. W.J. Wheatley left a pal behind: 'Clifford and I became good friends. Soon after his arrival we both joined the local scout group and we did most things together; roller skating, at the local rink, cinema visits, cycling and swimming, we also helped one another with our homework. The summers of 1940, '41 and '42 we spent most of our holiday on the local beach.'

Joyce Withers from Guernsey recounts her experiences of going home:

I was allowed to join the Brownies, and later the Girl Guides. I came home from such a meeting one evening to find Mr and Mrs Lanham having a 'special drink' they said, and asked had I heard the news? I hadn't heard anything – so they asked me to sit down and they would tell me. Apparently, they'd heard on the radio that the war was over – great rejoicing, hence the unusual drink. I was going to be able to return to Guernsey and my parents and brother and sister. I know I cried, probably a little happy to think I'd see my family again, but more because I didn't want to leave the Lanhams.

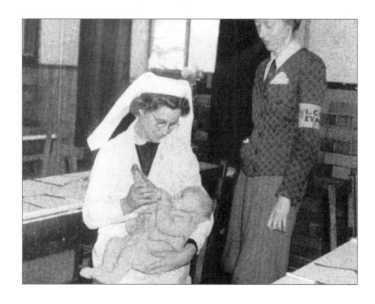

The return. A nurse and an evacuation helper with a returnee at Oliver Goldsmith dispersal point, 4 June 1945. (Crown Copyright)

Joyce Fry, six, and her brother Alec, eight, with their 'Auntie' (right) and her daughter outside their billet in Shepton Beauchamp, Somerset, in 1941.

One day I saw Mr Lanham doing some painting, in fact he was painting my name on my case, and my address in Guernsey. When I asked him why, he'd been told that my parents might not recognise me and I was to hold my case up in front of me on arrival on the island, so they would at least read my name and know I was their daughter. It came in useful. We first had to go through customs – I often wondered what they thought they'd find in our little cases! That completed, the big moment of looking for our parents came. I suddenly remembered that I didn't know who I was looking for, so I put my case up in front of me as I had been told to do. Then suddenly the people who were, I presumed, my family, came forward to greet me. Here I was saying 'Hello,' to a family I didn't know at all, and of course they didn't know me. Having established I was their daughter we all walked home.

But mostly, the homecoming was wonderful, as Anne Peppercorn recalls: 'At the end of the war my parents came to pick me up. That night Dad woke me up and took me over to the window, the fishing fleet was coming in with all their lights on; after all those years of blackout, it was a wonderful sight.' Eddie Roland has happy memories of seeing his family again: 'As we approached the harbour, we could see Dad on the upper walk. He was waving like mad. It was wonderful to see him, and astonishing how well he looked, thin, but tanned and fit. We disembarked and all walked home in a dream.'

Mr Beecher, Lewisham Education Officer, greets returning evacuees, June 1945. (Crown Copyright)

Joyce Fry remembers her return to Downham: 'I remember it was a freezing January day when I finally returned home. I rode on a tram which had its windows covered with a green criss-cross sticky material, so I couldn't see all those familiar sights that I had been so looking forward to seeing again. There were many laughs over the way I spoke, and the words I used, as I had a good bit of Somerset – "That be too hoigh for oi" – and then a bit of Yorkshire.'

It had been an event unlike any in modern history. A large part of a generation had been separated from their families during a part of their formative years. What legacy did their evacuation leave for the evacuees themselves? Perhaps this is best left to their own words:

June Cohen: 'Looking back now I think it broadened me and taught me how to mix with people of other denominations.'

Joyce Withers: 'You might get the impression that our lives were 'happy ever after'. Not so – my brother and I found difficulty in settling down. We were homesick for the places where we'd lived for the previous five years. I never liked my father, not a nice admission to make, but it's the truth. I left home at fifteen.'

Rozel Garnier: 'In a lot of ways it was a good thing; I learnt a lot, I saw another side of life and got a wider outlook. I can see things from another point of view.'

Phyllis Wilkins: 'I regret that time; it was a waste. My education could have been better; I failed the eleven plus – I just feel I could have made more of myself.'

George Powis: 'I know I was lucky, I call the people I got to love in Pontypool "God's Own" – they took in a boy and loved me. From them I learned to love the land, fresh food, and rugby!'

Roy Judge: 'I just read my way through evacuation. I just turned in on myself and read; detectives mainly.'

Vera Biddle: 'The lady of the house eventually became my "Aunty Cassie"; she was wonderful and treated me the same as her own two children. I have so many happy memories of that time. Aunty Cassie passed on a few years ago, though not before she came to see me married.'

Miriam McLeod: 'I see it as a time of real sadness – I just didn't want to be away from home. In 1941 we came back for the holidays; I remember the night before we went back I was physically sick. Later, I became very involved in the peace movement – I didn't want any other children to go through it.'

Caroline Williams: 'The evacuation certainly proved a success for someone – the teacher who was sent from my school met her future husband there.'

However much they might have wanted them to be, things could never be quite the same.

Eddie Roland: 'We left the island as children, and returned as adults. We had lived another life, had learned to look after

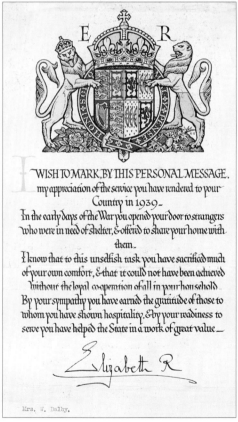

Jane Black: 'We received a card from the Queen Mother afterwards, thanking us for looking after the evacuees.' Of course, 'Elizabeth R' is now the Queen Mother.

ourselves and were used to a certain amount of independence. Dad still thought of us as children, under his authority, to stay around home and be obedient at all times. I was five inches taller than Dad and still growing. It required a lot of adjustment on all our parts and, in fact, we were never really the same people.'

Joyce Fry: 'It was stiff upper lip time, and it wouldn't do to let one's mates see any tears, but I think the effects went much deeper. I get much more upset now, thinking about these events, and sometimes get too choked to even mention them. I certainly have great respect for all those parents who had the courage to send their children away to safety, when it must have broken their hearts.'

One thing that struck me forcefully about so many of the people I interviewed was their incredible tolerance; even among those who had not been treated well, the majority sought to understand and excuse the people they had lived with.

Like all else, there are as many reactions as people, but there is one thing on which they are virtually unanimous. When I asked, 'If there was another evacuation, would you send your children away?', whatever their experience they nearly all replied – No!

Bibliography

BOOKS

Air Raid Protection: the Facts, Cambridge Scientists, 1938

Area Eight, Stroud and Nailsworth Defence Committee, 1945

August, Evelyn, *The Black-out Book*, George Harrap, 1939

Briggs, A. *The Channel Islands Occupation & Liberation*, Batsford, 1995

Briggs, S. *Keep Smiling Through*, Fontana, 1975

Calder, R. *The Lesson of London*, Secker & Warburg, 1941

Children in Wartime, Tressell Publications, 1989

Croydon and the Second World War, Croydon Corporation, 1949

Darwin, B. *War on the Line*, 1946

Essex at War, Essex County Standard, 1945

Falconer, D. and J. *Bath at War,* Sutton Publishing, 1999

Foster, R. *Dover Front*, Secker & Warburg, 1941

Haldane, J.B.S. *ARP*, Left Book Club, 1938

Hardy, C. *Hull at War*, Breedon Books, 1993

Knox, C. *The Unbeaten Track*, Cassell & Co., 1944

Lloyd's Under Fire, Lloyd's of London, 1945

London Transport Carried On, LPTB, 1947

The Metropolitan Police at War, HMSO, 1947

O'Brien, T.H. *Civil Defence*, HMSO, 1953

Ogley, B. *Surrey at War*, Froglets Publications, 1995

Ourselves in Wartime, Odhams, 1944

The Schools in Wartime, HMSO, 1941

Titmus, R.M. *Problems of Social Policy*, HMSO, 1950

Tragedy at Bethnal Green 1943, the Stationery Office, 1999

Twyford, H.P. *It Came to Our Door*, Underhill, 1946

Walker, J. *West Wickham in the Second World War*, Hollies, 1990

The War in East Sussex, Sussex Express and County Herald, 1945

The War over Walthamstow, Walthamstow Borough Council, 1945
Ward, S. *War in the Countryside*, Cameron Books, 1988
W*e Think You Ought to Go*, Corporation of London, 1995
Weir, Sir C. *Civilian Assignment*, Methuen & Co., 1953

NEWSPAPERS AND PAMPHLETS

Daily Express 1940
The Friends' Relief Service
Kentish Mercury 1942

GOVERNMENT PUBLICATIONS

Evacuation – Why and How?, July 1939
The Householder's Handbook, 1937
Notes for Billeting Officers and Voluntary Welfare Workers, 1941
The Protection of Your Home against Air Raids, 1938

Index